VISITORS'

SOUTH DEVON

STONE AGE TO COLD WAR

VISITORS' HISTORIC BRITAIN

SOUTH DEVON

STONE AGE TO COLD WAR

DEREK TAIT

PEN & SWORD
HISTORY

First published in Great Britain in 2018 by
Pen & Sword History
An imprint of
Pen & Sword Books Ltd
Yorkshire – Philadelphia

ISBN 978 1 52670 415 3

A CIP catalogue record for this book is
available from the British Library.

Printed and bound in England
By CPI Group (UK) Ltd, Croydon, CR0 4YY
Typeset by Aura Technology and Software Services, India

Pen & Sword Books Limited incorporates the imprints of Atlas, Archaeology, Aviation,
Discovery, Family History, Fiction, History, Maritime, Military, Military Classics,
Politics, Select, Transport, True Crime, Air World, Frontline Publishing, Leo Cooper,
Remember When, Seaforth Publishing, The Praetorian Press, Wharncliffe Local
History, Wharncliffe Transport, Wharncliffe True Crime and White Owl.

For a complete list of Pen & Sword titles please contact

PEN & SWORD BOOKS LIMITED
47 Church Street, Barnsley, South Yorkshire, S70 2AS, England
E-mail: enquiries@pen-and-sword.co.uk
Website: www.pen-and-sword.co.uk

Or
PEN AND SWORD BOOKS
1950 Lawrence Rd, Havertown, PA 19083, USA
E-mail: Uspen-and-sword@casematepublishers.com
Website: www.penandswordbooks.com

Contents

Introduction

South Devon is steeped in history. From the prehistoric caves at Cattedown in Plymouth to Bronze Age settlements, from relics of Roman occupation to Civil War battlefields and, from more recent times, the sites of American bases during the Second World War. All this and more can be found in this part of the county.

Roman presence has been recorded in Plymouth, Ipplepen and Dartmoor with pottery and many coins discovered in these areas. Previously, Roman occupation was thought not to have come any further than Exeter, but the numerous finds seem to disprove this. During the British Iron Age, the occupation of the Romans and early medieval times, Devon was the home of the Dumnonii Brythonic Celts. The name Devon derives from Dumnonia.

In the eighth and ninth centuries Dumnonia was partially assimilated into the Kingdom of Wessex and in 936AD, King Æthelstan set the western boundary with Cornwall at the River Tamar. Thereafter, Devon became a shire of the kingdom of England.

The south coast of Devon is made up of cliffs and sandy beaches containing holiday resorts, fishing towns and sea ports. Much of the inland terrain is rural and hilly with a low population density compared to many other parts of England. Dartmoor covers the largest open space in southern England stretching 368 square miles.

Human remains dating back 30,000 to 40,000 years have been discovered at Kent's Cavern and Dartmoor was inhabited by hunter-gatherers during Mesolithic times from 6,000 BC. Roman occupation covered a period of approximately 350 years. Saxon settlers first visited the area around 600AD with Devon becoming a frontier between Brittonic and Anglo-Saxon Wessex which was mainly absorbed into Wessex by the mid-ninth century.

During the 1600s strategic Civil War battles were fought at Plymouth, Sourton Down and Modbury and skirmishes occurred in various other parts of Devon before the capture of Dartmouth.

The area developed greatly over the centuries and, with the introduction of the railways in the 1800s, produce could easily be sent to other parts of the country while tourism increased greatly.

During the Second World War, Devon saw the arrival of thousands of American troops who trained and camped here before leaving for the beaches of Normandy on D-Day.

South Devon draws much of its income from agriculture and tourism and popular holiday destinations include Dartmoor, the English Riviera and the Jurassic Coast. Starting in Plymouth and travelling along the coast and inland areas of South Devon, ending at Sidmouth, this book recalls prehistoric settlements, vital battles during the Civil War, the important events leading up to D-Day and their embarkation points, famous people, events, disasters and the general trades and way of life of the people living in the area at the time.

CHAPTER 1

Plymouth

The beginning of our journey starts at **Plymouth.** The town's history stretches back to the Bronze Age and further; a settlement at Mount Batten became a trading post for the Roman Empire, later surpassed by Sutton, a village founded in the ninth century which later became Plymouth.

There is evidence to support the presence of Romans in the area. In 1894 a crock of Roman coins was discovered at Compton Gifford in Plymouth containing a thousand coins all dating from before 280AD. The British Museum suggested that it could have been part of a Roman pay chest for a legion stationed nearby. Romans are also believed to have once inhabited Stonehouse. The area carried the name Stonehouse even in Saxon times and it is believed that it was named after a ruin that, at the time, only the Romans could have built. Unfortunately, the ruin has long since disappeared.

In 1882 a Roman crematorium was discovered at Newport Street just below Stonehouse Bridge. It contained small tombs, about 4ft by 2ft, with human bones and ashes. Unfortunately, all were lost during the Blitz of the city during the Second World War. Evidence also suggests that Romans once inhabited the area, now called Roman Way (Roman Road is nearby) in St Budeaux. Roman Way was originally called 'Old Wall's Lane' which suggests an ancient occupation. A Roman signal station was believed to have once stood on the hill there and soapwort, which was used by the Romans for medicine, has been found growing nearby. Soapwort is usually only found in this country on the site of an old settlement.

Other evidence also points to the existence of Romans in the area. A galley was found at Newnham and Roman coins and pottery have been found at Mount Batten. In 1888 a large hoard of Roman coins was found at Stamford in Plymstock and a bronze figure of Mercury was found at Hooe.

The Ridgeway at Plympton has long been believed to be part of a Roman road. It is recorded in 1281 as Ryggeseweystrete and the strete part of its name suggests a Roman link. Records also exist of the discovery of early camps near Crownhill, although these may have been British. Roman coins have been discovered in the River Plym and at Whitleigh, Torr and Millbay, but these are few and far between.

In 1340 during the Hundred Years War, the area came under attack from the French who took prisoners and burned down a manor house, although they did not succeed in invading the town. However, in 1403 Breton raiders burned the town to the ground.

Plymouth Castle was built in the late 1400s near to the area now known as the Barbican. It had four round towers, one at each corner. Today, the castle is featured in the city's coat of arms. The castle protected Sutton Pool, which was the location of the naval fleet before the dockyard was built. Plymouth was further fortified after an Act of Parliament of 1512. Defensive walls were constructed at the entrance of Sutton Pool and a chain was stretched across the pool when the area came under threat.

On St Nicholas Island (later Drake's Island) defences were built to protect the town and six artillery blockhouses were constructed, including one at Fishers Nose towards the south-eastern corner of the Hoe. During the reign of Elizabeth I Sir Francis Drake reputedly played bowls on Plymouth Hoe in 1588 as the Spanish Armada was spotted in Plymouth Sound. At the time, Drake was vice admiral in command of the English fleet and the ensuing battle successfully defeated the Armada. In 1596 a fort (later known as Drake's Fort) was built for defence on Plymouth Hoe looking out towards the Sound.

In 1620 the Pilgrim Fathers left from Plymouth to set up colonies in the New World and their point of departure is marked by a monument on the Barbican.

Between 1642 and 1666, during the English Civil War, Plymouth was held by the Parliamentarians. The Citadel was constructed soon after, being built on the site of the earlier Drake's Fort.

The town grew during the Industrial Revolution and its port handled goods and passengers from the Americas as well as exporting local minerals such as tin, copper, china clay, lime and arsenic. The nearby town of Devonport grew up around the dockyard and became a vital shipbuilding and naval port.

In 1914, Plymouth, Devonport and Stonehouse (the three towns) amalgamated into one single town, Plymouth which achieved city status in 1928. The town's strategic naval base made it a target for enemy aircraft during the Second World War and the city suffered from extensive, heavy bombing. The Blitz destroyed the city which was completely rebuilt after the war.

Standing on **Plymouth Hoe** and looking out into the Sound, it's possible to see the incredible history that surrounds the area. **Drake's Island** (named after Sir Francis Drake and formerly known as St Nicholas Island) is the site of an extinct volcano. The island is a giant plug which seals off the vent of this once active volcano. Across the water in Cornwall, the shores of Kingsand are made up of a purple volcanic rock called Rhyolite. A close inspection of the rock shows that some of it contains thousands of gas bubbles from the volcano's last eruption. Rhyolite is a rock formed by the solidification of molten magma. The last eruption took place a very long time ago; the Rhyolite dates from the Permian Period (299 – 251 million years ago) and represents a geologic period which included the diversification of early amniotes into the predecessors of mammals, turtles, lepidosaurs and archosaurs. It is the last period of the Paleozoic Era and included the largest mass extinction known to science. Ninety per cent of all marine species became extinct, as did seventy per cent of all land organisms.

Smeaton's Tower on Plymouth Hoe which was erected originally on the Eddystone Reef in 1759.

Smeaton's Tower is the key landmark on Plymouth Hoe. It was built by John Smeaton on the Eddystone Reef in 1759. There had been two previous lighthouses there, the first built by Henry Winstanley in 1695. Unfortunately, seven years later during a storm it was washed away taking its builder with it. The second lighthouse was built in 1711 by John Rudyerd but was destroyed by a fire in 1755. Work commenced on Smeaton's Tower in December 1756 to replace the damaged lighthouse. Smeaton's Tower would still be there today if the rock underneath had not been undermined by the sea. James Douglass built a new lighthouse on an adjoining rock and it was felt that if

Smeaton's Tower was left standing beside the new lighthouse, it could eventually collapse onto it if the rock beneath it became even more undermined. It was decided to blow it up but a Mr F.J. Webb suggested that it should be dismantled and erected on the Hoe where the Trinity House Navigational Obelisk once stood. This was quite a task and the lighthouse was removed stone by stone and rebuilt on the Hoe with a new base to support it. The original base can still be seen out to sea, beside the present Eddystone Lighthouse. On 24 September 1884 the Lord Mayor opened Smeaton's Tower on the Hoe to the public.

Further towards **West Hoe** is the spot where the *Titanic* survivors returned to Plymouth. On 28 April 1912 they were brought back to Millbay Docks, fourteen days after their ship sank after colliding with an iceberg on her maiden voyage from Southampton to New York. At 8am the SS *Lapland* moored at Cawsand Bay with the 167 members of the *Titanic* who hadn't been detained in New York for the American inquiry. Three tenders left Millbay Docks to collect the passengers and the 1,927 sacks of mail that had been scheduled to be carried by the *Titanic*. The third tender, the *Sir Richard Grenville*, carrying the survivors, killed time in the Sound while the dock labourers and porters were paid off and escorted out of the dock gates at West Hoe. After midday the tender was given the all clear and the survivors were allowed to disembark in an air of secrecy. They were then put on a special train from Millbay Docks to Southampton where they arrived at 10.10pm that night.

Plymouth Hoe is also the site where the last public execution in the town took place. Between the Naval Memorial and the Hoe Lodge Gardens, there is a cross with the number '3' embedded in the pavement. This marks the spot where three Royal Marines were executed by firing squad on 6 July 1797. Their names were Lee, Coffy and Branning and they were found guilty of attempting to incite a mutiny at Stonehouse Barracks. Another marine, M. Gennis, was convicted of a similar crime and sentenced to 1,000 lashes and transported to Botany Bay for life.

Ten thousand men of the Fleet and garrison were brought to watch the mutineers die and most of Plymouth also turned out. When the three men faced the firing squad and the shots were fired, Coffy and Branning fell forward, dead, into their coffins. However, Lee was not hit and had to go through the whole procedure again. The reserve firing squad lined up, took aim and fired, but again Lee was untouched. Once more, they loaded, took aim but again missed Lee. Finally, a sergeant came up behind him and shot him dead at close range. Earlier fourteen seamen had been hanged at the yardarm on their ships in the Sound. This was to be Plymouth's last public execution.

Nearby places of interest:
Smeaton's Tower is open daily between 10am to 5pm. There are excellent views looking towards Plymouth, the Barbican and out into the Sound from the top of the tower. Phone: 01752 304774.

3 Elliot Terrace was once home to Nancy Astor. She received many well-known visitors at the house including Winston Churchill, George Bernard Shaw, Noël Coward and Charlie Chaplin. Today, the premises are licensed for civil ceremonies and partnerships, commitment ceremonies, re-affirmation of vows and naming ceremonies. Group tours also take place there. Phone: 01752 304858. Email: lordmayor@plymouth.gov.uk

Tinside Lido is one of the few remaining art-deco lidos in the UK. Well maintained, it is popular with swimmers during the summer months and is open between May and September. Phone: 01752 261915.

Travelling down from the Hoe, the visitor arrives at the **Barbican.**

Stand anywhere on the Barbican and you will be looking back into history. The narrow lanes were once the home to seafarers such as

A vintage photo showing New Street on the Barbican. The Elizabethan House can be found at number 32 and the Elizabethan Gardens at number 34. The street also houses cafés, galleries and public houses.

Francis Drake, Walter Raleigh, John Hawkins and Captain James Cook. Walk the back streets and you are walking through areas where Britain's heroes once trod. New Street on the Barbican is the home to the Elizabethan House which is preserved and decorated as it would have been in the 1600s.

A memorial recording the leaving place of the Pilgrim Fathers for America in 1620 can be found on the quayside and thousands of

A view of the Barbican from the harbour. On the left of the photo is the Admiral MacBride Inn, said to be the location of the original point where the Pilgrim Fathers left for America in 1620.

people visit the spot every year. The Mayflower Steps were only built in 1934 and the actual leaving spot is some distance further back as much of the harbour was reclaimed and built many years later. As unbelievable as it sounds, the actual leaving place of the Pilgrims can be found in the ladies' toilet of a nearby pub, The Admiral MacBride.

Nearby places of interest:
The Elizabethan House *at 32 New Street is a well-preserved house showing how a merchant or sea captain might have lived in the 1600s. Phone: 01752 344840.*

Chris Robinson's Plymouth Prints *at 34 New Street. Author and local historian, Chris Robinson's shop sells books, videos, prints and DVDs of the history of Plymouth. Phone: 01752 228120. Email: chris@chrisrobinson.co.uk*

The Merchant's House *at 33 St Andrew's Street is Plymouth's finest surviving example of a sixteenth and seventeenth century home. It contains a museum various historical artefacts including a seventeenth-century Trelawney mantelpiece, gold-painted nineteenth century shop front signs, a doll's house from the 1870s, a ducking stool, local truncheons and manacles and a mock-up of a Victorian school room. Phone: 01752 304774.*

The National Marine Aquarium *houses the largest public aquarium in the UK visited by 300,000 people each year. Attractions include sharks, octopus and a huge variety of different marine species. Opens daily between 10am and 5pm. Phone: 0844 893 7938. Email: enquiries@national-aquarium.co.uk*

The Mayflower Steps *are open all year around and feature a portico complete with Doric columns made of Portland stone which was constructed in 1934. It commemorates the leaving place of the*

Pilgrim Fathers in 1620, although the actual leaving point was further back. Phone: 01752 773549.

The South West Image Bank *is located at 25 Parade on the Barbican and opens on Tuesdays and Wednesdays between 10am to 4pm. The Image Bank contains a huge collection of photos of the area dating back to the 1870s. Phone: 01752 665445. Email: clare@southwestimagebank.com*

The Plymouth Gin Distillery *is the only remaining distillery in Plymouth and is located in what was once a Dominican monastery which was originally built in 1431. The distillery has been open since 1793 and is located at 60 Southside Street. Regular tours take place. There is a very popular bar and bistro above the distillery. Phone: 01752 665292.*

The Dolphin Inn, *or Dolphin Hotel, dates from the early nineteenth century and was the setting for many of Beryl Cook's paintings. The Grade II listed building is linked with several of the Tolpuddle Martyrs who stayed at the hotel in 1838 when they returned from exile in Australia. Phone: 01752 660876.*

Looking out towards **Cattedown** large oil containers can be seen. It's hard to imagine that the area was once inhabited by prehistoric beasts. The story of Cattedown Man is well-known and his remains were discovered in limestone caves in the Cattedown area of the city in 1887. With him were the bones of fifteen early humans together with the remains of woolly rhinoceros, woolly mammoth, deer and lion, all dating from the Ice Age. The remains were approximately 140,000 years old and are the oldest discovered in the British Isles. Prehistoric remains have also been found in Ernesettle Woods, at Mutley and Keyham as well as at Stonehouse. Because of the fuel depot, the caverns at Cattedown are off limits to the general public.

The British naval officer and explorer Robert Falcon Scott was born in Plymouth on 6 June 1868. He led two expeditions to Antarctica.

The first, the *Discovery* Expedition began in 1901 and lasted three years. His second, the *Terra Nova* Expedition, which commenced in 1910, is better known and was where, unfortunately, he lost his life. Scott led a team of five men in a race to reach the South Pole. When he arrived on 17 January 1912, he discovered that he had been beaten to the Pole by the Norwegian, Roald Amundsen and his team. Scott and his team, which included Edward Wilson, H.R. Bowers, Lawrence Oates and Edgar Evans, made their way back, but died of a combination of cold, hunger and exhaustion.

Scott was born at Outlands House, the family home, in the Parish of Stoke Damerel. He was a distant descendant of Sir Walter Scott and the father of the naturalist, Peter Scott. Outlands has now gone and St Bartholomew's Church on Outlands Road stands in its place. Within the church is a piece of wood bearing Scott's name. In 1908 Scott had carved his name on a tree at Outlands, from where the wood was taken.

Scott was 43 when he died and his body, and that of his comrades, remain at the camp where he was found. A wooden cross was erected on top of a high cairn of snow which covered the camp. A memorial stands to Scott at **Mount Wise** in Devonport.

Across the Sound can be seen a pier jutting out into the water, from a rocky outcrop known as **Mount Batten,** named after Sir William Batten (c.1600-1667), MP and Surveyor of the Navy.

T.E. Lawrence – Lawrence of Arabia – was stationed at Mount Batten in Plymouth and was posted to RAF Cattewater during March 1929. He stayed in Plymouth until 1935 where he worked on high-speed boats. Previously, at the beginning of the First World War, Lawrence had been a university post-graduate researcher and had travelled extensively within the Ottoman Empire. When he volunteered his services, he was posted to Cairo where he fought with the Arab troops against the enemy forces of the Ottoman Empire. In 1918 he was involved in the capture of Damascus and was promoted to lieutenant colonel. After the war his fame spread, so when he joined the RAF in 1922 he enlisted as John Hume Ross to protect his identity. This was discovered in 1923 and he was forced out of the RAF. He changed his name to T.E. Shaw and joined the Royal Tank Corps but was unhappy there and petitioned the RAF to re-accept him, which they did in 1925. He died aged 46 in a motor bike accident near his cottage in Wareham.

There is a plaque at **Turnchapel** which commemorates Lawrence. It reads:

Lawrence of Arabia 1888-1935.

On his return from India in 1929 T.E. Lawrence, under the assumed name of Shaw, was posted to a flying boat squadron at RAF Mount Batten. He remained in the marine craft section until his discharge 19 February 1935.

The history of Mount Batten dates much further back and there is evidence that the earliest trade with Europe took place there in the late Bronze Age. Trade continued through the Iron Age period and the Roman occupation. Ancient finds along the peninsula include three British-made bronze mirrors as well as other items. Unfortunately, these were all destroyed in the Blitz. Much of Plymouth city centre today contains buildings built after the Second World War because of the bombing. However, on the Barbican there are buildings dating from Tudor times such as the Elizabethan House and the Merchant's House.

Heading away from the centre of Plymouth towards **Stonehouse** is Union Street, the home of the old Palace Theatre, which today is in a state of disrepair. Stars who appeared there in the past included Charlie Chaplin, Harry Houdini, Laurel and Hardy and Lillie Langtry. Harry Houdini famously jumped from the nearby Stonehouse Bridge (Halfpenny Bridge) in chains and padlocks.

Travelling further along Union Street and turning into Durnford Street, the traveller finds himself in the street where Sir Arthur Conan Doyle once stayed. He assisted at a medical practice at Durnford Street and Sherlock Holmes was said to be based on his

The Palace Theatre in Union Street, Plymouth, where Harry Houdini, Laurel and Hardy and Charlie Chaplin once appeared.

colleague, Dr Budd. Conan Doyle achieved the titles of Bachelor of Medicine and Master of Surgery in 1881 and had studied with George Turnavine Budd at Edinburgh. When Budd opened a practice in Durnford Street in 1882, he asked Conan Doyle to join him but the partnership didn't last long. Although Budd and Conan Doyle were friends, Conan Doyle found his partner over-prescribed drugs for his patients, for which he charged them and was unorthodox in the extreme. He wrote and told his mother Mary about Budd's ways. She had never been an admirer of his. After two months, the partnership was dissolved because Budd said that it was short of both finances and patients. Conan Doyle discovered later that Budd had found one of his letters to his mother and the real reason for the break up of the partnership was that he had been upset by what he had read.

Conan Doyle left and set up a practice in Southsea with just £10 to his name. At first, it was not very successful and while he was waiting for patients he wrote his first story featuring Sherlock Holmes, *A Study in Scarlet*.

The house in Durnford Street where Admiral Hardy once lived. Vice Admiral Horatio Nelson famously said to him 'Kiss me, Hardy' as he lay fatally wounded aboard HMS Victory *in 1805.*

Conan Doyle died on 7 July 1930, aged 71. Today, passages from his works featuring Sherlock Holmes can be found on brass plaques set into the pavement at Durnford Street.

Further along, at 156 Durnford Street is the house where Vice Admiral Sir Thomas Masterman Hardy once lived. A plaque marks the spot. Although he rose through the ranks to become a vice admiral, his Naval career is remembered by just three words, 'Kiss me Hardy'. When Vice Admiral Horatio Nelson was fatally wounded aboard HMS *Victory* in 1805, he was taken below deck where he was later visited by Hardy. Nelson's words to him were, 'Take care of poor Lady Hamilton', before he uttered the immortal words, 'Kiss me, Hardy'. It has been suggested that what Nelson actually said was, 'Kismet, Hardy' meaning that this was his fate. However, that was not the case as many officers present, including his surgeon, William Beatty, who wrote down his words, bore witness to the actual event. When Nelson uttered the words, 'Kiss me, Hardy', Hardy knelt beside him and kissed him on the cheek. Many people think that these were his last words but his final words were uttered just before he died three hours after he had been shot. These words were, 'God and my country'.

A young sailor from Cawsand, Lieutenant John Pollard, was a midshipman on the *Victory* when Nelson was fatally wounded. Although not a well-known name now, it was Pollard who shot and killed the enemy sailor who shot Nelson. He was known thereafter as 'Nelson's Avenger'. However, several other men also claimed to have shot the Frenchman.

Following Durnford Street to its end, the visitor next comes to **Devil's Point** with views of Plymouth Sound and Cornwall. A walk to the right eventually leads to Royal William Yard which, today, is the home to many restaurants and bars. Before reaching William Yard, a plaque on a low wall commemorates the sailing of Charles Darwin on board HMS *Beagle*, who left from across the bay at Barn Pool on the Mount Edgcumbe estate.

The Royal William Yard in Stonehouse. Today, it is the home to restaurants, bars and art galleries.

Darwin lived in Plymouth for two months before his famous voyage around the world in HMS *Beagle*. The ship was captained by Robert Fitzroy. Darwin, who was then just 22 years old, joined the crew as a naturalist. He had a wealthy family who paid the £30 fare needed to travel on the ship.

When he returned to England, he married Emma Wedgwood, the daughter of the potter, Josiah Wedgwood. He carried on his research and in 1859, his book *The Origin of the Species by Means of Natural Selection* was published.

Darwin died in 1882 at his home in Orpington, Kent. He is buried at Westminster Abbey.

Nearby places of interest:
156 Durnford Street, *once home to Vice Admiral Sir Thomas Masterman Hardy. Nelson famously said to Hardy as he lay dying, 'Kiss me, Hardy'.*

The Cremyll Ferry, which allows foot passengers to visit the picturesque Mount Edgcumbe Estate across the water in Cornwall, is located at Admiral's Hard at Stonehouse. Phone: 01752 822105. Email: info@plymouthboattrips.co.uk

The Royal William Yard was designed by Sir John Rennie and was constructed between 1825 and 1831. Steeped in history, today it is the home to many restaurants, bars and cafés.

Devil's Point, at the end of Durnford Street, features scenic walks, giving views of the Hoe and the Sound. At the eastern end, the walk leads on to Royal William Yard.

CHAPTER 2

Plympton to Newton Abbot

The Plympton to Newton Abbot route can be taken by following the A38 (the Devon Expressway) which from Ivybridge skirts the edge of Dartmoor. Along the way there are Neolithic, Celtic and Saxon settlements to be discovered, Iron Age and Norman castles, abbeys, remnants of a Roman past, the sites of Civil War battles, American troops in the Second World War and the tale of a man upon whom Arthur Conan Doyle's novel *The Hound of the Baskervilles* was based.

A vintage photo showing the empty streets of the Ridgeway in Plympton. Today, the area bustles with shops and pedestrians.

The first stop on the route is **Plympton.** During prehistoric times Celtic settlements could be found in the area of Plympton. A nearby settlement, **Bury Down**, which means 'Earth Work on the Hill', later became Boringdon. **Boringdon Camp,** an Iron Age and Roman earthwork in Cann Woods, is a Scheduled Monument. The site consists of a castle circle which measures approximately 500ft.

In the Domesday Book in 1086, Plympton is described:

The King holds Plympton. TRE [Latin for Tempore Regis Edwardi which translates to 'in the time of King Edward'] *it paid geld for two and a half hides. There is land for 20 ploughs. In demesne are two ploughs and six slaves and 5 villans and 12 bordars with 12 ploughs. There are 6 acres (24,000 m²) of meadow and 20 acres (81,000 m²) of pasture, woodland one league long and a half broad. It renders £13 10s by weight. Beside this land the canons of the same manor hold 2 hides. There is land for 6 ploughs. There 12 v have 4 ploughs. It is worth 35 shillings.*

Plympton was once an ancient stannary town and a major trading centre for locally mined tin. It was also a seaport which was supplied by the River Plym. When the Plym silted up, trade moved further down the river to Plymouth.

Close to School Lane and Barbican Road in Plympton are the remains of a castle which can be found on top of a purpose built mound. At one time a deep river led straight up to the castle which allowed ships to take local tin to destinations worldwide. In the thirteenth and fourteenth centuries, Plympton St Maurice was larger and a more important port than nearby Plymouth. A lot of silt was produced by the tin mines on Dartmoor and this eventually led to the river becoming silted up. The area of Valley Road leading to Plympton St Maurice was all under water 600 years ago.

An ancient settlement built by the Damnonii once stood where **Plympton Castle** stands today. Their defences were later fortified by the Romans. During the ninth century, the Saxons built a small wooden fort at Plympton to defend themselves during raids on the south coast by the Danish. The area was given over to Richard de Redvers, the Earl of Devon, after the Norman Conquest and he built a motte-and-bailey castle there some time in the early 1100s. During the civil war for the English throne between 1135 and 1144, his son Baldwin sided with the Empress Matilda against King Stephen in 1136 and Stephen sent a large force of men to the castle who seized it and burnt it the ground. Five years after the event Baldwin had the castle rebuilt in stone in a circular shape on top of the motte.

In 1204 the castle was confiscated by King John and, through marriage, eventually belonged to Fawkes de Breauté, a soldier and royal servant who had been knighted in 1207. When the king died in 1216, de Breauté swore his loyalties to Henry III and fought at the Battle of Lincoln where rebel barons, together with Prince Louis of France, had planned to defeat the king. When de Breauté later argued with Hubert de Burgh, the Earl of Kent and one of the king's key magnates, it resulted in his loss of power and in 1224, de Burgh ordered him to give up both the castle at Plympton as well as one at Bedford. De Breauté refused and King Henry sent an army to take the castle which fell after fifteen days. De Breauté fled overseas and into exile.

In the early twelfth century William Warelwast founded Plympton Priory. Its members were all Augustinian canons and the priory was the second richest monastic house in Devon. In 1872 it was noted that the gatehouse, kitchen and refectory were still in good condition, however today only the gatehouse still exists.

Dedicated in 1311, St Mary's Church was originally a parish chapel attached to Plympton Priory. There are monuments to members of the Strode family which include a tomb-chest for Richard Strode (d. 1464), with his effigy clad in armour. The monument of William Strode (d. 1637) and his family depicts a husband, two wives and ten children. There is also a monument of W. Seymour (d. 1801) in Coade stone and to the 11-year-old heir to the Earl of Morley of Saltram House, Viscount Boringdon, who died in Paris in 1817.

The Church of St Thomas at Plympton St Maurice is Norman in origin and features a tower which was rebuilt in the fifteenth century.

Plympton was held by the Royalists during the Civil War and Prince Maurice had his headquarters at the castle in 1643, although nearby Plymouth was staunchly Parliamentarian. In 1644 Maurice's troops were forced to withdraw and the castle fell into disrepair thereafter.

The artist Sir Joshua Reynolds was born in the town in 1723. He later became Mayor of Plympton and was the first president of the Royal Academy of Art. His father was headmaster of Plympton Grammar School which still exists but is now known as Hele's School.

Nearby places of interest:

Plympton Castle located on Barbican Road, Plympton. The ruins of the former fortification still remain. Previously, the Saxons had built a small wooden fort at the same location during the ninth century.

Saltram is a National Trust property which includes acres of land together with a café, tea room and gift shop. It is very popular with walkers and cyclists and includes an abundance of wildlife. Saltram House is a grade I listed mansion house dating from the George II period and is open to the general public daily. Phone: 01752 333500. Email: saltram@nationaltrust.org.uk

Plym Valley Railway is a restored heritage railway covering 1½ miles and includes a section of what was once part of the South Devon and Tavistock Railway, a branch line of the Great Western Railway. The railway is based at Coypool Road and the journey extends to Plymbridge Woods. Phone: 07580 689380. Email: plymrail@yahoo.co.uk

The old part of **Plympton St Maurice** in Fore Street includes a collection of buildings and homes dating back to the 1600s and before. The Guildhall, built in 1688, is where Sir Joshua Reynolds presided as mayor in the council chamber upstairs. The Guildhall was once used as a court and included two cells with stocks and a ducking stool used on offenders. A short walk away can be found Plympton Castle. Channel 4's Time Team visited the area in 1998.

Following the Devon Expressway, the visitor passes Lee Mill before coming to the town of Ivybridge.

Ivybridge first appears in records in 1280 and was described as a dowry of land, west of the River Erme, by the Ivy Bridge (from where the town took its name).

Power was generated by the local river and a tin mill, an edge mill, a tool mill and a corn mill prospered in the 1500s. Later, a tucking mill, for cloth-making, and two paper mills were constructed. The water leats channeled the water direct into the mills.

A ghostly apparition is connected to the popular Longtimber Woods. In the fifteenth century Tom Treneman, who was an employee at Stowford House, was killed when he fell off his horse. After his funeral he appeared to a servant boy who was so shocked

The bridge at Ivybridge which gave the village its name. The town was first mentioned in records in 1280.

that he died of fright. Twelve parsons were called and put a halter around the ghost's neck before leading him to Black Anne Pool on the River Erme. Treneman's pool still spooks many people today with mysterious and sometimes ludicrous tales of his ghost.

By the 1700s the town housed a small community built up around the London Hotel, a coaching inn on the Plymouth to Exeter route.

In June 1913 the Great Women's Suffrage Pilgrimage picnic was held in Victoria Park, Ivybridge while the women were on their way from Cornwall to London.

During the First World War Belgian refugees were housed at Rutt Cottage, Ivybridge, in February 1915. In September that year, a thousand sandbags were sent to the front from the town.

In 1916 a British airship crashed close to Ivybridge but the pilot survived the ordeal. During December 1917 Stowford Lodge opened as a V.A. Auxiliary Hospital. A war memorial to those lost in battle during the First World War was unveiled in 1922.

During the Second World War American troops were billeted at Ivybridge in readiness for the Normandy landings in 1944. The troops formed part of the 29th Division which had a gas and fuel supply depot at Wrangaton. The GIs of the 116th Infantry Regiment were first stationed in Ivybridge in May 1943. They were part of Operation Bolero which involved transferring and accommodating nearly two million British and American soldiers in preparation for D-Day. The 116th Infantry Regiment contained men from all over America but each detachment had a significant number of men from the National Guard unit in Virginia. The 29th Division left Tidworth in Wiltshire and marched to Devon and Cornwall as part of Exercise Hanover. Their new barracks in Ivybridge awaited them.

Only the 1st Battalion of the 116th Regiment, commanded by Colonel Charles Draper Canham, was stationed at Ivybridge. The battalion stayed in the town for a year while training, part of which involved marching and camping on the moors, whatever the weather. Training started at 5am and went on until 5pm, excluding Sunday.

The American camp was based at Uphill on Exeter Road and consisted of Nissen huts behind a wire fence. Each hut contained twelve bunk beds and could house twenty-four men. There was also a cinema, a canteen, workshops and a jail as well as gymnasiums complete with games pitches outside. There were so many Americans stationed in Ivybridge that the population doubled which was a godsend to the small shops and many public houses in the area.

During Christmas 1943 the American soldiers laid on parties for local children where they were given sweets and gifts. Children from the surrounding areas were also invited. The Americans were well-loved in the town and are remembered for their generosity and kindness. Many became good friends with the locals. When the troops left for D-Day the town seemed empty, devoid of all the busyness of the troops and their machinery.

Italian and German prisoners of war were also brought to Ivybridge and made to work on the land until the late 1940s.

Today, there is a memorial in the town which honours the American soldiers who were once stationed there. It can be found at Harford Road car park. An inscription on the memorial reads:

Dedicated to all the American Servicemen based in Ivybridge 1943-1944 particularly the 1st Battalion 116th Infantry Regiment who made many friends with local residents. Sadly many of these men were to die on, or after, D-Day the 6th June 1944.

There are also memorial benches to the Bedford Boys in MacAndrews Field, which is now a recreational area but once formed part of Uphill Camp. The Bedford Boys was an affectionate name given to the soldiers of the small town of Bedford, Virginia who were part of Company A, 29th Infantry Division. They were in the first wave of American soldiers to land on Omaha Beach on D-Day and nineteen were killed in the first minutes, three during the later fighting.

Nearby places of interest:
Dartmoor Zoo *at Sparkwell is open every day of the year apart from Christmas Day. In the Summer (April to October), the opening times are 10am to 6pm and in the Winter (October to April), the opening times are 10am to 4pm. The zoo includes a variety of animals including a Siberian tiger, an African lion, a Jaguar, a Syrian Brown Bear together with many other mammals and a variety of birds. The zoo featured in the book and movie, 'We Bought a Zoo'. Phone: 01752 837645. Email: zoobase@dartmoorzoo.co.uk*

Endsleigh Garden Centre *at Ivybridge opens from Monday to Saturday from 9am to 6pm and on Sunday from 10.30am to 4.30pm. It also includes a popular restaurant. Phone: 0844 288 5093.*

The Donkey Sanctuary *is located at Filham Park, Godwell Lane in Ivybridge and opens on most days between 9am until dusk. Admission and parking are free. Phone: 01752 690200.*

The village of **North Huish** lies east of the Devon Expressway between Ugborough and Avonwick. The manor was held by John Damarell in the reign of King Richard I (1189-1199) and for many generations by his male descendants. It later passed into the hands of the Trenchard family before being owned by Tremain of Collacombe. St Mary's Church within the village was built in the fourteenth century and enlarged during the fifteenth century. Bishop Grandisson dedicated the church on 15 June 1336. Its spire dates from medieval times.

The small village of **Rattery** is found on the east of the Devon Highway. Rattery is a variation of its original name 'Red Tree' and had nothing to do with a dwelling for rats. In the Domesday book it is listed as Ratreu. The Saxons knew it as Ratrew.

The famous seventeenth century poet Robert Herrick lived at nearby **Dean Prior**. He was the vicar there between 1629 to 1646 and 1660 to 1674 and is buried in an unmarked grave in the village. The church contains a Norman font together with a fine carved wooden screen.

Nearby places of interest:
The Church House Inn *dates back to the sixteenth century although there has been a building on the site since 1028. The inn serves food and drink and has its own restaurant. A friendly ghost is said to be in residence but is rarely seen. Phone: 01364 642 220.*

Buckfastleigh can be found to the west of the Devon Expressway. This small market town on the edge of Dartmoor lies within the Totnes Deanery. Buckfast, the home of Buckfast Abbey is one mile to the north.

'Buckfast' means 'stronghold' and would have been an area where deer and bucks were kept. 'Leigh' refers to the pasture belonging to Buckfast. In the eleventh century, King Canute, who famously tried to hold back the sea, established the Benedictine Abbey at Buckfast. The original abbey was built in 1018 but its exact location is unknown although it was described as 'small and unprosperous'. In 1134 the abbey was established in its current position and housed Savignac monks. King Stephen had previously granted Buckfast to the French Abbot of Savigny. In 1147 the abbey became a Cistercian monastery after the Savignac congregation merged with the Cistercians. Soon after the monastery was built of stone. During medieval times the abbey grew rich due to the trade in sheep wool and through fishing. The Black Death killed two abbots and many monks and by 1377, only fourteen monks remained at the abbey. However, Buckfast became one of the wealthiest abbeys in the south west and owned its own sheep runs on Dartmoor and fisheries on the Dart and Avon, as well as seventeen manors in Devon together with townhouses in Exeter and a dwelling for the abbot at Kingsbridge.

Its fortunes waned in the sixteenth century and between 1500 and 1539, just twenty-two monks were ordained. By the time of

An old photo showing Buckfast Abbey. The original abbey was built in 1018 but its exact location is unknown. The present abbey was built in 1134 and housed Savignac monks.

the abbey's dissolution, there were only ten monks left. After the Dissolution of the Monasteries, Abbot Gabriel Donne surrendered the abbey to Sir William Petre, an agent for King Henry VIII, in 1539. Soon after, he received a large annual pension of £120 which he received until his death in 1558.

During the Industrial Revolution the town grew with the introduction of woollen, paper and corn mills. The railway line to Buckfastleigh was constructed by the Buckfastleigh, Totnes and South Devon Railway and opened in May 1872.

The woollen mills in the town were owned by the Hamlyn family up until 1920. In 1887 they built a new Town Hall and community building in celebration of Queen Victoria's Golden Jubilee. They were also responsible for building new cottages for workers in the town.

Nearby places of interest:
Buckfast Abbey *has free entry all year round and features a book shop, gardens, gift shop and restaurant. Phone: 01364 645500.*

The South Devon Steam Railway *(formerly known as The Dart Valley Railway) features a 7-mile line that allows visitors the chance to travel on a vintage steam train. Phone: 01364 644370. Email: trains@southdevonrailway.org*

Pennywell Farm and Wildlife Centre *opens every day from 10am to 5pm. It features a variety of farm animals as well as play areas, games and activities. Phone: 01364 642023*

The Buckfastleigh Butterfly Farm and Otter Sanctuary, *located at the Steam and Leisure Park, Buckfastleigh, features otters, butterflies and terrapins and includes free parking, a café and picnic areas. The sanctuary opens from 10 am to 5pm. Phone: 01364 642916. Email: contact@ottersandbutterflies.co.uk*

The Tomb of Squire Richard Cabell *lies within the grounds of Buckfastleigh Church. Phone: 01364 643212.*

The Valiant Soldier *was formerly a popular pub in Buckfastleigh. It closed in the late 1960s and everything was left untouched. Today, it is open as a museum and allows visitors to relive a slice of the past. Phone: 01364 644 522. Email: whowasthevaliantsoldier@ gmail.com*

Staverton to the east of Buckfastleigh features a fourteenth century church, the church of St Paul de Leon. Features within the building include the restored rood screen, an eighteenth-century pulpit and a monument to the Worth family dating from 1629.

Nearby is **Staverton Bridge** which dates from 1413 and spans the River Dart. It is thought to be one of the finest examples of medieval bridges surviving today in Devon.

In West Buckfastleigh lies **Brook.** In 1656, Richard Cabell built the manor house of Brook. He died in 1677 and local legend records that, on the night of his death, large black hounds breathing fire, ran over Dartmoor and surrounded Cabell's house, howling incessantly. His unusual tomb was said to be designed to stop his restless spirit roaming the moor.

The Hound of the Baskervilles, the novel by Sir Arthur Conan Doyle, was based on this legend. Doyle's friend Bertram Fletcher Robinson, who lived at Ipplepen, reputedly first told him about the legend of the Dartmoor hound. The book was published in 1902. The carriage driver for the Fletcher Robinson family was named Harry Baskerville. Other nearby places mentioned in the book include Princetown and Bellever Tor, both on Dartmoor.

An older photo of North Street in Ashburton showing a policeman and another man directing the then almost non-existent traffic.

Ashburton is recorded in the Domesday book as Essebretone. The town lies on the south-southeastern edge of Dartmoor beside the A38. During the English Civil War, Royalist troops took refuge at Ashburton after being defeated by General Fairfax at Bovey Tracey. The old Mermaid Inn can be found at 4 North Street and is said to be where Thomas Fairfax stayed for one night.

In 1845 shot, weighing four pounds, from the Civil War period, was found in an old tree near Buckfast Abbey, which was in ruins at the time. When builders were renovating the Royal Oak Inn, a rubbish bag split open and a musket ball rolled out. When the rest of the contents were checked, it was found that they contained several small grey military tunic buttons, a leather double buckle military belt, four musket balls, three clay pipe bowls, one of which had a military insignia.

During the Napoleonic Wars, Ashburton (along with others) was designated a parole town where prisoners of war could live amongst the residents, provided they agreed to abide by certain rules. French prisoners were also allowed to live in a similar way with the locals at Bodmin, Callington, Tavistock and Tiverton. One of the rules stated that 'the prisoner is allowed to walk within one mile of the town centre but he must not enter open land or road'. One mile from the town is a stone called the Parole Stone which remains there today and marks the spot to which prisoners were allowed to travel.

In August 1795 there were 300 French prisoners on parole in Ashburton, which made the area, to locals, appear more like a French town than an English one. All were well-dressed and the government allowed the officers half a guinea and the men 5s 3d per week. Also in 1795 William Sunter, who was a magistrate in Ashburton, wrote a letter to Robert Mackreth, the town's MP. He was concerned that the number of French prisoners in the town was soon to increase to 500. He asked the MP to suggest to the Admiralty that the men should be moved to towns further away from the coast. He stated that there were insufficient provisions for the locals as it was and an increase in prisoners would only make matters worse.

In 1854 the figurehead from the French frigate *La Virginie* could be found in the north aisle of St Andrew's Church. The vessel which had been captained by M. Bergeret and had been taken by Lord Exmouth on 20 April 1796. Captain Bergeret was a parole prisoner at Ashburton at the time.

Several men and boys from the town fought at the Battle of Trafalgar. These included John Ball, aged 15; William Ferris, aged 17; John Murch, aged 19; John Murch, aged 40; Robert Pengalley, aged 27; William Pengalley, aged 24; Robert Smerdon, aged 20; Richard Webber, aged 50; Robert Whiteway, aged 38 and Andrew Wickham, aged 30.

In 1807 Danish prisoners of war were detained on two ships, *The Prince* and *El Firme* before being sent on parole to Ashburton and other towns.

The wars with France and America caused a problem of what to do with captured prisoners. Previously they had been kept on ships or hulks but in 1806 it was decided to build a prison on Dartmoor to house them. The prison at Princetown was completed in 1809 and housed all the French prisoners. Americans were interred there in 1812. Captured Americans from the US ship *Chesapeake* were allowed to wander freely on parole in Ashburton after the ship's capture in 1813. In 1814, Andrew McDonald, who was a captured captain of the land forces, was released from parole at Ashburton and allowed to return to America on the proviso that he didn't engage in any action that added to the hostilities between Britain and America.

Nearby places of interest:
River Dart Country Park is located at Holne Park in Ashburton and includes 90 acres of park land as well as a camp site. There are also various attractions and walks. Phone: 01364 652511. Email: info@ riverdart.co.uk

Hill House Nursery and Garden at Landscove, Ashburton, features a family run plant nursery set in six acres. Phone: 01803 762273. Email: bluebird@hillhousenursery.com

Ashburton Museum is located at the Bull Ring and is open between 2pm and 4pm on Tuesday, Thursday and Friday and between 10am and 12am on Saturday. Phone: 01364 652539. Email: museum@ ashburton.org

Bovey Tracey is a small town on the edge of Dartmoor and describes itself as 'The Gateway to the Moor'. The town was established during Saxon times and takes its name from the River Bovey. In the Domesday Book the town is named 'Bovi'. The Tracey part of the name comes from the de Tracey family who, after the Norman Conquest, were lords of the manor. The full name first appears in records in 1309.

In 1170 a member of the de Tracey family, William, was involved in the murder of Archbishop Thomas Becket at Canterbury Cathedral. It is said, as penance, that he was made responsible for the rebuilding of the parish church of St Peter, St Paul and St Thomas of Canterbury. A borough was created at Bovey Tracey in the early thirteenth century by Henry de Tracey and, in 1259, he was granted the right to hold a weekly market and an annual three-day fair.

On 9 January 1646 Oliver Cromwell and his Roundhead troops arrived at Bovey Tracey at night, catching Lord Wentworth's Regiment by surprise. Many Royalist troops from Wentworth's army escaped but 400 horses were captured. It is said that the Royalists managed to escape by throwing coins from their windows while the poorly paid Roundhead troops were distracted picking them up. The next day, the Cavaliers (Royalists) and the Roundheads (Parliamentarians) fought a battle on nearby Bovey Heath. Cromwell's army succeeded in defeating the Royalists. Today, the local pub is called 'The Cromwell Arms' and a nearby stone arch is known locally as 'Cromwell's Arch'.

Nearby places of interest:
The House of Marbles is a museum which explores the 4,000 year history of glass. It features games and activities for children as well as a large picnic area. Phone: 01626 835285.

Bovey Heath stretches for 50 acres and today is designated a Site of Special Scientific Interest; it has been a Devon Wildlife Trust nature reserve since 2002 and a Local Nature Reserve since 2003. The heath was created 4,000 years ago by Bronze Age farmers who cleared large area of woodland so that it could be used for grazing and the cultivation of crops. At least one Bronze Age tumulus stands on the site.

As previously mentioned, the Battle of Bovey Heath took place here during the English Civil War in January 1646. Two earthworks, dating from this period, can be found on the site.

In the nineteenth and twentieth century, much of the heath was destroyed by open-cast mining for ball clay. In the Second World War American troops trained on the site in readiness for D-Day.

Ipplepen is a small village situated approximately 3.7 miles to the south-west of the market town of Newton Abbot. The site of an important Roman cemetery which included fifteen skeletons, was discovered in the village by metal detectorists and an archaeological

A vintage shot showing the village of Ipplepen. Bertram Fletcher Robinson, a friend of Sir Arthur Conan Doyle, lived at Ipplepen and reputedly first told him about the legend of the Dartmoor hound which later featured in his book, Hound of the Baskervilles.

dig took place in the early part of 2015. One skeleton showed that the settlement was still being used for as much as 350 years after the end of the Roman period in 410AD.

Nearby places of interest:
St Andrew's Church *dates from 1450. The village stocks still remain in the churchyard.*

Parkhill House *in Ipplepen is where Sir Arthur Conan Doyle once stayed while gathering ideas for his book, 'The Hound of the Baskervilles'. The house belonged to his friend, Fletcher Robinson, whose father's coachman was called Harry Baskerville.*

The market town of **Newton Abbot** on the River Teign has a population of approximately 26,000. At Berry's Wood Hill Fort near Bradley Manor, traces of people from Neolithic times have been

St Leonard's Tower in Newton Abbot. The tower is all that remains of a medieval chapel.

discovered. The contour hill fort that once stood there, enclosed 11 acres. Some time before the first century, Milber Down camp was built. It was later occupied by the Romans and coins dating to this period have been found there.

On Highweek Hill is Castle Dyke which features the remains of a Norman motte-and-bailey castle. A village grew up around the castle and was originally known as Teignwick. This later became Highweek which meant 'the village on the high ground'. A second village was built on the low ground near to the River Lemon and eventually became part of Wolborough Manor.

Nearby places of interest:

Trago Mills *at Newton Abbot features a large range of discounted household and garden items. It also has a picnic area as well as several cafés, a restaurant, landscaped gardens and other independent shops. Phone: 01626 821111.*

Decoy Country Park *was originally a clay quarry but today has lakes and ponds which support a host of wildlife. Water sports activities also take place and there is a large children's play area together with a water play feature. Phone: 01626 361101. Email: info@newtonabbot24.co.uk*

Bradley Manor House *belongs to the National Trust and dates to medieval times. It is set amongst meadows and woodland in the valley of the River Lemon. Much of the house was built by Richard and Joan Yarde who were the owners from 1402. In 1938, Mrs A.H. Woolner, the daughter of the Egyptologist Cecil Mallaby Firth, gave Bradley to the National Trust. Phone: 01803 661907.*

North of Newton Abbot is **Kingsteignton.** The town was founded in the eighth century by the kings of Wessex and formed the centre of an extensive Saxon estate which stretched from Teignmouth to Manaton. In Saxon times Kingsteignton was a major settlement.

In 1001, Danish raiders plundered the town which provided rich pickings.

The Manor of Kingsteignton was a crown demesne until the thirteenth century. It passed on to the Clifford family in 1509, the title of Lord of the Manor is still held by the family today. In medieval times prosperity led to the rebuilding of St Michael's Parish Church in the 1400s. Its tower, measuring 85ft, was constructed in the 1480s. Until the 1850s the parish church was the mother church of Highweek and Newton Bushell. The Fairwater Leat fed a water supply to the town in the Middle Ages as well as supplying the power for three mills.

In 1791 Josiah Wedgwood first purchased Kingsteignton clay. Fine quality ball clay beds were created between 30 to 40 million years previously during the Oligocene Period. These lie on the eastern edge of the Bovey Basin near Kingsteignton and were first exploited in the late 1600s, primarily for pipe making. Potters were attracted to their white firing properties and this attracted the interest of Wedgwood. Over the following 200 years, clay mining brought prosperity to the town and created many jobs. Limestone was also quarried there at various times and stone from Kingsteignton Quarry at Rydon was used for the building of Buckfast Abbey. Today, the town is twinned with Orbec in France.

Nearby places of interest:
Stover Country Park *covers an area of 114 acres and includes a woodland with a lake together with marshland, wildlife, a heritage trail, nature interpretation centre arboretum, a raised forest boardwalk, carved seats and Ted Hughes poetry boards. It is located on the A382 Newton Abbot to Bovey Tracey road. Tel: 01626 835236. Email: stover@devon.gov.uk*

The Stover Canal *was first opened in 1792 and used to transport clay until it closed in the early 1940s. In 1999, the Stover Canal Society* *was founded to preserve and maintain it so that it can be enjoyed by visitors and the local community. Email: info@stovercanal.co.uk*

Ugbrooke House *was mentioned in the Domesday book of 1086. It has been the seat of the Clifford family for over 400 years. The house and gardens are located in Chudleigh and are open on certain days throughout the summer. There is also an Orangery tearoom serving light snacks and cream teas. Phone: 01626 852179. Email: info@ ugbrooke.co.uk*

CHAPTER 3

Dartmoor

Dartmoor covers a huge expanse of land and includes prehistoric settlements, standing stones, the infamous Dartmoor Prison, high tors, rivers and beautiful reservoirs. It has National Park status and covers an area of 368 square miles. The south of Dartmoor covers the area from Yelverton to Bovey Tracy and includes Tavistock, Princetown, Dartmeet and Widecombe-in-the-Moor. To the north are Lydford, Okehampton, Belstone, Drewsteignton and Moretonhampstead.

Many of the prehistoric remains found on Dartmoor date back to the Neolithic and early Bronze Ages. Dartmoor has the largest concentration of Bronze Age remains in the United Kingdom. At one time the moorland was covered in trees but these were cut down and removed by prehistoric settlers so that the land could be used for farming. Fire was used to clear much of the land and over many centuries, this led to acidification of the soil as well as the accumulation of peat and bogs in the area. The climate in those times was much warmer than it is today, but over thousands of years the climate grew colder and the areas were abandoned. Today, it remains much the same and due to the acidic soil, there are no organic remains. However, the granite buildings, enclosures and monuments, together with flint tools have survived.

Approaching Dartmoor from Plymouth, **Yelverton** is found on the A386. It is a small village with shops, a public house and a petrol station. In the nineteenth century a railway station opened in the village and brought commuters and tourists from nearby Plymouth. The Great Western Railway line originally ran to Tavistock.

Dartmoor ponies can be found roaming all over Dartmoor. Numbers have declined in recent years. In the 1930s, there was an estimated 26,000 but today only approximately 800 ponies are known to be grazing on the moor.

A view of Yelverton looking towards the Rock. RAF Harrowbeer once flew planes from this spot during the Second World War.

Across the road is a disused runway which was formerly RAF Harrowbeer. During the Second World War the airfield was used for air defence against German attacks on Devonport Dockyard and the Western Approaches. Today, the runways can still be seen but it is not obviously apparent that the area was once used as an airfield. Bunkers built of earth and brick still remain. These were used to protect fighters against attack on the ground. For many years, much to the delight of small boys, they remained open and it was possible, even in the 1970s, to find old bullet cases and other souvenirs. Today, however, they are sealed up.

The shops in the main part of the village were once a terrace of nineteenth century houses. The upper floor of the buildings were removed to make landing on the runway an easier task. Nearby St Paul's Church was not altered but its tower was hit by a plane

The small village of Yelverton at the beginning of Dartmoor. A garage, grocery store and café can be found amongst the shops on the right hand side of the photo.

and a warning light was later installed. Some American airmen were stationed at Harrowbeer during the war and a plane carrying the US president, Franklin D. Roosevelt, landed during this time.

A rock at the beginning of the runway has been popular with climbers for many years. Known locally as Yelverton Rock, families enjoying an ice cream nearby are happy to let their children climb it. The rock is also known as Roborough Rock but has also, in the past, been known as the Duke of Wellington's Nose or George III's nose as well as Ullestor Rock or Ulster Rock. In the 1500s, it was known as Udell Torre and also Udal Tor. On a map of 1765 it appeared as Hurstone Rock. The nearby public house The Rock Hotel takes its name from the prominent stone. Yelverton Rock used to be larger but the middle section was removed in 1830 for road maintenance.

Nearby places of interest:
Buckland Abbey *is a National Trust property which is open to the public for much of the year. It was once the home of Sir Francis Drake. The Plymouth City Museum and Art Gallery house some of their collection there. It is also the home to Drake's Drum which he took with him when he circumnavigated the world. Phone: 01822 853607.*

The Garden House *at Buckland Monachorum is open during 31 March to 31 October, daily between 10.30am and 5pm. It includes 10 acres of well-kept gardens together with a café. Top quality plants can be bought at reasonable prices. Phone: 01822 854769. Email: office@thegardenhouse.org.uk*

Powdermills Pottery *is located within granite buildings that once were part of a nineteenth century gunpowder factory. The pottery has its own resident potter, Joss Hibbs, as well as a shop. During the summer season, cream teas are served in the courtyard. The pottery is located off the B3212 in between Two Bridges and Postbridge. Phone: 01822 880263.*

To the south of Yelverton is **Shaugh Prior.** The area is rich in Bronze Age monuments which include cists and cairns. Tin mining also took place in the parish as did the mining of china clay at the nearby Lee Moor. The church in the village, dedicated to St Edward, was originally built in the eleventh century although the present building, complete with granite tower, dates from the fifteenth century.

An American general, Joseph Palmer, who fought during the American Revolutionary War was born in Shaugh Prior in 1716. John Phillips (1835–97) who was the founder of the Aller Vale Pottery in Kingskerswell was also born there.

A walk through the woods leads uphill towards the rocky outcrop, the Dewerstone. From this high point, it is possible to look for miles across Dartmoor. Passing the Dewerstone and following the track by the River Plym, there are the remains of a quarry tramway as well as several quarries with heaps of waste rock.

North-east of Shaugh Prior is the **Brisworthy** stone circle. The circle has a diameter of 24 metres and consists of twenty-four upright stones, all less than a metre tall. Over the years, most of the stones toppled over but in 1909, they were restored to their original positions. Fifteen of the original forty stones are missing and were probably taken by local farmers and used in walls and enclosures.

Away from the Rivers Plym and Meavy, the land rises 600ft to **Wigford Down** where many prehistoric stone structures can be found including enclosures, stone ramparts belonging to a prehistoric fort as well as hut circles. The area was mined for tin in the sixteenth century and leats and reservoirs associated with the industry can be seen. Clay mining also took place in the nineteenth century.

There is much to be seen by the walker taking a route from Dewerstone towards **Cadover Bridge**. The road from Cadover Bridge leads back to Yelverton where the B312 leads towards **Dousland** and out towards open moor, eventually leading to Princetown, the home of Dartmoor Prison. Burrator Road at Dousland takes the visitor to the picturesque **Burrator Reservoir** and the village of **Sheepstor.**

The reservoir was completed in 1898 and enlarged in 1929. Today, it is very popular with tourists, walkers, joggers and cyclists. A variety of animals have been spotted in the area including deer and wild boars and fishing permits are available. Burrator Reservoir features in the Al Pacino movie *Revolution* (1985) as well as in Steven Spielberg's movie *War Horse* (2011).

The road from Burrator leads back to the B312 and on to **Princetown**. The village was established in 1785 when the Secretary to the Prince of Wales, Sir Thomas Tyrwhitt, arranged to lease an area of Dartmoor hoping to use it as farmland. He encouraged people to live there and suggested that a new prison should be built there. He called the village Princetown after the Prince of Wales.

Dartmoor Prison, which was completed in 1806, originally housed thousands of prisoners from the Napoleonic Wars and the later war of 1812. A small town built up around the prison with many residents finding work there. The prison closed in 1816 and the town nearly collapsed but was regenerated when the Dartmoor Railway opened in 1823 bringing many workers to the granite quarries. The prison re-opened in 1851 to house inmates serving long sentences.

The village was once served by the Princetown Railway but this was closed in 1956. It was, at the time, the highest railway line in England. Today the tracks have been removed but the old line is popular with walkers and cyclists with the route leading to Foggin Tor where an old granite quarry can be found. The area is very picturesque with steep sloping granite hills and a small lake. Sir Arthur Conan Doyle made the area famous in his novel *The Hound of the Baskervilles* and nearby Fox Tor Mires is believed to be the site of the Grimpen Mire mentioned in the book.

Continuing past Princetown, the road continues to a crossroads at Two Bridges. Taking the road left leads to **Rundlestone, Merrivale** and **Tavistock.**

Nearby places of interest:
The Dartmoor Prison Museum *is located opposite the main gates of the prison at Princetown and opens between 9.30am and 4.30pm on Mondays, Tuesdays, Wednesdays, Thursdays and Saturdays. It features a range of exhibits relating to the prison and its prisoners. Phone: 01822 322130.*

The National Park Visitor Centre *is located on Tavistock Road at Princetown. It includes exhibitions relating to the area as well as a conservation garden and a children's discovery zone. Phone: 01822 890414. Email: visit@dartmoor.gov.uk*

Wistman's Wood, near Two Bridges, contains the remains of the ancient forest that once covered much of Dartmoor in 7000BC. It was cleared by Mesolithic hunter/gatherers some time around 5000BC. The oldest oak trees are about 400 to 500 years old. It is a short walk from the car park at Two Bridges.

Merrivale is situated on the B3357 where the River Walkham crosses. A large spoil tip from the remains of Merrivale granite quarry can be seen on one side of the road. Nearby are a few houses built originally for quarry workers as well as the Dartmoor Inn.

Above Merrivale and to the south-east of the hamlet are a stone circle a stone row and a standing stone measuring 3.8 metres.

On either side of a stream, two stone avenues run parallel to each other with the remains of a barrow at its centre. Further south of the stone avenues is a large kistvaen (tomb or burial chamber). It once contained a flint scraper, a number of flint flakes and a whetstone for polishing metal items. Unfortunately, some time in the past, the top of the cist has been broken in two by a farmer who would have used it to make a gatepost. Several tors can be seen from the spot including King's Tor and Staple Tor.

North of Merrivale is the Langstone Moor Stone Circle. It was restored in 1894 when all the stones which had toppled over were re-erected. For many years the stone circle was quite impressive, but unfortunately American troops used the stones for target practice during the Second World War. Today only three of the original stones remain standing with another ten overturned or completely destroyed. Originally the circle contained sixteen stones and measured 20.9 metres. The nearby Langstone standing stone, which stands almost 3 metres tall, still carries the marks of the American army's bullet holes. Caution should be taken if visiting the Langstone standing stone as it falls within the Merrivale live firing range which is used today for military training.

The river and bridge at Tavistock. Bronze and Iron Age remains exist close to the town and it is believed that an older settlement once existed on the site of Tavistock.

Tavistock, at the end of the B3357, is an ancient stannary and market town and dates back to the tenth century. Sir Francis Drake was born nearby. Bronze and Iron Age remains can be found in the surrounding area and it is believed that an older settlement existed on the site of Tavistock. In 961AD, the abbey of Saint Mary and Saint Rumon was founded by Ordgar, the Earl of Devon. It was destroyed by Danish raiders in 997AD but was later restored. Amongst its well-known abbots was Aldred, who crowned Harold II and William I, and was the Archbishop of York when he died.

Henry I granted a Royal Charter in 1105 which allowed the monks to run a weekly Pannier Market. A three-day fair was introduced in 1116 to celebrate the feast of Saint Rumon. The tradition is carried on today and the event is known as Goosey Fair.

Tavistock achieved borough status in 1185 and by 1295 had become a parliamentary borough, with two members sent to parliament. In 1285 the abbey church was rebuilt and in 1305 Edward I issued a charter making Tavistock one of four stannary towns where tin was stamped and weighed. Monthly courts were held to regulate mining affairs.

Sir Francis Drake was born around 1540 at Crowndale Farm; a Blue Plaque marks the spot on the current farmhouse, although the original farmhouse was dismantled and the stone transported for use in Lew Trenchard. There is a statue of Drake at the beginning of Tavistock and an exact copy also appears on Plymouth Hoe.

Nearby, copper, manganese, lead, silver and tin were mined and the town had a considerable trade in cattle and corn, together with brewing and iron-founding.

In the seventeenth century the cloth trade took over from a waning tin trade. The town remained prosperous under the stewardship of the Russells. When the Black Death arrived in 1625, fifty-two townspeople died of the disease.

During the Civil War the town was held by the Parliamentarians in 1642 before being taken by the Royalist troops the following year after the defeat of the Parliamentary forces at Braddock Down.

The cloth market was starting to wane by 1800 but copper was starting to be mined in the area and by 1817 the Tavistock Canal had been dug out. Most of the labour came from French prisoners of war. Via the canal, copper was carried to **Morwellham Quay** on the River Tamar and was loaded on to sailing ships.

In 1859 Tavistock was connected to the Great Western Railway and the London and South Western Railway. The centre of the town was redesigned and included a new town hall and the Pannier Market buildings. Abbey Bridge was widened and a new Drake Road continued from Bedford Square to the LSWR station. The town's population grew to 9,000 but by 1901, this had halved. The railway closed in 1968 following the Beeching Report.

The branch to the right of Two Bridges leads to Hexworthy, Dartmeet, Buckland-in-the-Moor and Widecombe-in-the-Moor. Following the road further leads to Haytor Vale and Manaton.

Nearby places of interest:
Tavistock Pannier Market *lies behind the town hall and is open daily every Tuesday to Saturday between 9am and 4.30pm. A wide range of crafts, food and other goods are available. Phone: 01822 611003.*

Tavistock Farmers' Market *is held on the 2nd, 4th and 5th Saturday of each month in Bedford Square. It offers a wide variety of locally produced food, drink and plants. Phone: 07785538153. E-mail: info@tavistockfarmersmarket.com*

Tavistock Museum *is located in the historic Court Gate with the entrance being in Guildhall Square. It is opens daily between 11am and 3pm from Easter Saturday until the end of October. Phone: 01822 611264. Email: info@tavistockmuseum.co.uk*

Tavistock Trout Farm and Fishery *lies on the edge of Dartmoor and includes seven holiday cottages and apartments complete with their own pub, The Trout 'n' Tipple. Facilities include the Oak Gazebo with barbeque, a children's play area, five fly fishing lakes, a float fishing lake and a tackle shop. Phone: 01822 615441. Email: abigail@ tavistocktroutfishery.co.uk*

Hexworthy is a small hamlet on the West Dart River. The Forest Inn opened in the 1850s. On the opposite bank of the river can be found the hamlet of **Huccaby** which has a parish church dedicated to St Raphael. Hexworthy has a long history of tin mining and nearby tin works were recorded in 1240.

The **Down Ridge Stone Circle** (or Hexworthy Stone Circle) lies to the south of Hexworthy. The circle measures 25 metres in diameter and features five upright stones, standing at a height of 1.45 metres, with six more stones lying where they've fallen over. In 1904 the site was partially excavated by the Dartmoor Exploration Committee revealing a ground surface covered in charcoal. Approximately 85 metres south-east of the stone circle is an associated triangular shaped rock which stands 0.86 metres high.

Further north-west stands the **Sherberton Stone Circle** which originally would have measured 30 metres in diameter. Nine stones still remain standing measuring up to 0.75 metres. The two fallen stones measure approximately 2.5 metres.

Dartmeet lies towards the end of the B3351 road and is a popular tourist spot. The road continues past Poundsgate and over Holne Bridge and New Bridge to Ashburton on the edge of Dartmoor. Dartmeet has an important archaeological landscape due to its prehistoric field systems which are delineated by reaves (boundary walls) and are amongst the best preserved in north-west Europe. Crossing the river is an ancient clapper bridge which, today, is partially collapsed.

Coffin Stone lies halfway up Dartmeet Hill. Coffins were placed here by bearers while they rested before burial services at Widecombe-in-the-Moor. The rock is in two pieces and legend states that God struck the stone with a thunderbolt when the coffin carrying the body of an evil man was rested there.

Nearby places of interest:
Pixieland can be found on the way to Dartmeet and includes a range of goods including local produce, books, clothing and jewellery. A pixie garden, complete with toadstools, allows the visitor to have their photo dressed as a pixie while sat on one of the colourful toadstools. Phone: 01364 631412.

Adventure Clydesdale offers the chance to ride Clydesdale horses over Dartmoor on trail riding holidays. They are based at Brimpts Farm near Dartmeet. Phone: 01364 631683 (evenings), Mobile: 07809 729739 or 07901 943038. Email: info@adventureclydesdale.com

Buckland-in-the-Moor is a small village with a population of about 90. Near to the church is a view point called Buckland Beacon. The Ten Commandments can be found there carved in stone. Mr W.A. Clements, a stonemason from Exeter, was engaged by the Lord of Buckland Manor, Mr Whitley, to engrave the granite stones in 1927.

Widecombe-in-the-Moor is a small village which is well-known for Widecombe Fair which is held yearly and includes the folksong, 'Old Uncle Tom Cobley and All'. The words to the song were originally published in 1880. Much of the village's income comes from tourism and there are several gift shops and two cafés together with two inns, the Old Inn and the Rugglestone.

The church in the village is dedicated to St Pancras and was built in the fourteenth century using local stone. In 1638 it was severely damaged during the Great Thunderstorm when it was hit by ball lightning during an afternoon service. Four of the 300 worshippers were killed and sixty more were injured. Legend says that the church was visited by the devil who caused the destruction.

Novelist Beatrice Chase is buried in the churchyard. She claimed to be a direct descendant of William Parr, the brother of Catherine, the sixth wife of Henry VIII. Chase's birth name was Olive Katharine Parr.

Near to the village is Hutholes, a deserted medieval village, as well as the abandoned farmstead Dinna Clerks. Five miles away from the village is the Rippon Tor Rifle Range.

Following the road from Widecombe leads to the impressive tor at Haytor. The movie *Knights of the Round Table* starring Robert Taylor and Ava Gardner was filmed there in 1953 and an elaborate and impressive castle was constructed between the two main rocks of the tor where medieval jousting was staged.

To the north-west of Haytor is the atmospheric Hound Tor, said to be the inspiration for Sir Arthur Conan Doyle's *Hound of the Baskervilles*. Nearby is Hundatora, a deserted medieval village. The village was built on land farmed in the Bronze Age and was probably used in Roman times. There is a prehistoric farmstead approximately

400 metres north-west of the deserted village and to the south are several Bronze Age hut circles as well as outlines of medieval fields.

The Little Hound Tor (or White Moor) Stone Circle is in good condition and measures 20.2 metres in diameter. In 1896 only thirteen stones remained standing but another five were re-erected by the Dartmoor Exploration Committee in that year. In 1974 Tom Baker filmed the *Doctor Who* serial *The Sontaran Experiment* at Hound Tor.

Taking the road straight on from Two Bridges leads to **Bellever** and **Postbridge** before ending up at **Moretonhampstead.**

Bellever is a small hamlet situated on the River Dart. The first recording of a settlement there comes from 1355. The hamlet

The clapper bridge at Postbridge. The bridge is thought to have been constructed in the thirteenth century to allow pack horses to cross the river to carry tin to the stannary town of Tavistock.

originally consisted of Bellever Farm and its outbuildings together with a few cottages for farm workers. In 1931 the Forestry Commission purchased the farm and started a large planting scheme and in the 1950s several houses were built to house forestry workers. Today the coniferous plantation is known as Bellever Forest and it surrounds the hamlet on its north, west and south sides and is a popular destination for walkers.

Postbridge is a small picturesque village which is popular with tourists because of its clapper bridge. The bridge was first recorded in the fourteenth century but is thought to have been constructed in the thirteenth century to allow pack horses to cross the river. They were needed to carry tin to the stannary town of Tavistock. Today the clapper bridge is a Grade 2 listed structure. It stands beside another bridge which was built in the 1780s.

The B3212 road between Postbridge and Two Bridges is infamous as the location for the legend of the Hairy Hands. Since 1910 the disembodied hands are said to have grabbed the steering wheels of cars or handlebars of bicycles causing them to crash. In June 1921 Dr E.H. Helby, the medical officer for Dartmoor Prison, died after losing control of his motorcycle combination while on the road. The children of the prison governor, who were riding in his sidecar, survived the crash. Several weeks later a coach driver lost control of his vehicle and several passengers were thrown from of their seats. The tale reached London newspapers on 26 August 1921 when an army captain told how a pair of invisible hands had forced his motorcycle off the road.

Jay's Grave (or Kitty Jay's Grave) lies to the east of Postbridge near to Manaton. Buried there is a suicide victim who died in the late eighteenth century. The grave is well-known and has become the subject of local folklore as well as several ghost stories.

The little burial mound lies at the side of a small road, approximately a mile north-west of Hound Tor. It is close to the entrance to a green

Cows grazing beside Hound Tor. A deserted medieval village called Hundatora was built on land farmed in the Bronze Age and was probably used in Roman times.

lane leading to Natsworthy. At regular intervals, fresh flowers are laid on the grave but the person placing them there is never seen.

To the north of Postbridge is the Grey Wethers Stone Circles which consists of a pair of circles, both approximately 33 metres in diameter. Each circle consists of thirty stones. An excavation of the site took place in 1898 and charcoal fragments were found within the circles. In 1909 the circles were restored and fallen stones were re-erected.

Close by is the **Warren House Inn** which stands alone in the heart of Dartmoor. It is the highest pub above sea level in southern England and is located on an ancient road that crosses the moor, about 2 miles north-east of Postbridge. The present public house dates from 1845 but an older inn dating from the 1700s once stood across the way before it burnt down. The earliest recorded landlord was William Tapper who ran the inn in 1786.

Folklore tells of a local farmer at the inn who was persuaded to buy a flock of sheep after a night's drinking. However, the following morning, he discovered that the 'sheep' he'd been shown the previous night were actually the prehistoric stone circles at Grey Wethers. It is said that the fire in the hearth has never been allowed to go out and that the glowing embers of the fire from the original inn were taken across the road on a shovel to the hearth of the new building.

Further north, **Moretonhampstead** is a market town with a population of about 3,000. It is recorded in the Domesday Book of 1086 as Mortone, which is Old English for a farmstead in moorland. The Hampstead part of its name was added in 1493.

Shortly after 682AD the area was occupied by the Saxons and it was split into several vast estates. These estates included all the land within the boundaries of the rivers Teign and Bovey. Moreton became its main settlement.

After the Norman Conquest of 1066 it stayed a royal estate and is mentioned in the Domesday Book. During the reign of King Edward I (1272-1307) the manor was held by Richard de Burgh, the 2nd Earl of Ulster (1259–1326). For the privilege he had to pay the sum of one sparrowhawk yearly. It later became the seat of Sir Philip de Courtenay who was killed at the Battle of Stirling in 1314.

In later years, wool and the making of woollen cloth became the town's major industry and lasted for over 700 years. In the thirteenth century a water-powered fueling mill was built. In 1207 King John decreed that a weekly market and an annual five-day fair could be held in the town. This signified that Moretonhampstead had become a major local community. Throughout the Middle Ages the town grew and stayed prosperous due to its wool industry, until the seventeenth century. Although the industry declined, the town remained a local trading centre and a stop-off point for travellers crossing Dartmoor to and from Exeter and Newton Abbot.

During the twentieth century a number of fires destroyed many of the ancient buildings, but fortunately many survived.

George Parker Bidder (1806-1878) was born in Mortenhampstead. Known as 'the calculating boy', he was a maths prodigy who was exhibited at fairs by his father and later became an engineer..

Nearby places of interest:

The Moretonhampstead Motor Museum *has a collection of over 100 vintage vehicles including carts, motorbikes and cars as well as other memorabilia relating to motoring. The museum is open from Thursday to Monday between 11.30am and 4.30pm. Phone: 01647 440 636. Email: moretonhampsteadmotormuseum@gmail.com*

The Dartmoor Hawking Falconry Experience *is set in 40 acres on the Bovey Castle estate and is a private falconry centre which is not open to the general public but allows private clients to enjoy falconry as part of an interactive and personal experience. Tel: 07791560948 Email: info@dartmoorhawking.co.uk*

At **Sourton Down** on 25 April 1643 Sir Ralph Hopton, together with his Cornish army, marched toward Okehampton as the Parliamentarians fled from Launceston. Hopton hoped to strike a decisive blow, but Major General Chudleigh led a small force of cavalry and ambushed the Royalists at Sourton Down near the edge of Dartmoor. A charge against the advance guard of Royalist dragoons was led by Captain Drake and the men panicked and fell back before running into the troops behind.

The Parliamentarians continued their attack and routed half the Royalist army. Lord Mohun and Sir Bevil Grenville tried to defend the artillery while Hopton relayed orders to Sir Nicholas Slanning to bring up the rearguard. The Parliamentarian attack was finally forced back which led to the Royalists taking up defensive positions amongst the ancient earthworks on Dartmoor. Chudleigh, together with 1,000 foot soldiers from Okehampton, continued to attack the Royalists and fighting carried on into the night. The Royalists eventually withdrew leaving behind weapons, gunpowder and other stores. The Parliamentarians managed to capture Sir Ralph Hopton's portmanteau, containing communications from the king commanding the Cornish army to join forces with the Marquis of Hertford and Prince Maurice in Somerset.

CHAPTER 4

Bovisand to Bigbury-on-Sea

The road from Bovisand to Bigbury covers a beautiful part of the South Devon coast with stunning beaches. **Bovisand** has two beaches as well as a holiday park. The northern-most beach is known as Bovisand Bay, while the southerly beach is Crownhill Bay. Nearby is Fort Bovisand which was constructed during the 1860s to defend the entrance to Plymouth Sound. In 1816 a stone jetty and slipway were built so boats from warships could land and collect fresh water from the nearby reservoir. In 1845 the first fort at the site was built and still remains; it is known as Staddon Heights Battery. Construction of the present fort was completed in 1869 and originally housed twenty-two 9-inch Rifled Muzzle Loaders together with one 10-inch RML gun. There was accommodation for up to 180 men.

The fort was used during the Second World War and in 1943 a Bofors 40mm anti-aircraft gun was installed there. In 1956 the Ministry of Defence abandoned the site but in 1970, the fort was leased and became a scuba diving centre and the home of a diving school. The company went in to liquidation in 2000.

Further along from Bovisand, and within walking distance, is **Heybrook Bay.** Overlooking the bay is the Eddystone Inn. From this area there are beautiful views overlooking the sea to Plymouth and Cornwall. Seals and dolphins are often spotted from the rocks near to the beach.

Around the coast from Heybrook Bay is **Wembury** which was visited by Mesolithic man; flint implements have been found nearby as well as Roman coins. The area was colonised by the Saxons in the seventh century who managed agricultural settlements in the area.

An older photo showing a carter and men at Wembury. The Mewstone can be seen in the background.

In 851AD, the Danes were repelled at Wembury. The church was dedicated to Saint Werburgh, a Saxon saint.

At **Wembury Point** are the remains of HMS *Cambridge*. In the 1930s, the area was the location of a busy and very popular holiday camp. The Southern Railway Handbook of 1936 carried an advert for the camp and described it as 'a smaller type camp with that family holiday atmosphere'. The camp boasted a licensed club, excellent food and cooking and comfortable bedrooms. Pastimes included cricket, tennis, dancing and table tennis. The advert also stated that the camp was 'on 100 acres by the sea with its own riding stables, safe bathing and good fishing'. There was accommodation for 150 and the cost to stay started at 35 shillings a week. It came to an end at the beginning of the war.

In 1940 a gunnery range was established at Wembury, together with a radar station, observation posts and anti-aircraft guns.

A view of the Mewstone and Wembury Point, once the home to HMS Cambridge. *Today the area is owned by the National Trust.*

The whole area was later acquired by the Navy in 1950. In 1956 the HMS *Cambridge* Gunnery School was established at Wembury Point and was finally closed in 2001. In 2006, the National Trust turned the area into a nature reserve.

Out to sea, off the shores of Wembury, stands the **Mewstone,** a spectacular wedge-shaped island, owned by the National Trust. In 1744 a local man was found guilty of a petty crime and was 'transported' to the island for seven years where he lived peacefully with his family. When he returned to the mainland, his daughter, known locally as 'Black Joan', decided to remain behind. She later married and had three children before her husband was killed falling off a rock.

In 1813 the artist J.M.W. Turner landed on the Mewstone and made several sketches of the island. In 1833 a man called Samuel Wakeham settled on the island with his family while living a dual life as a smuggler. Basking sharks can sometimes be spotted out by the Mewstone.

The Mewstone at sunset as seen from Wembury beach. In 1813 the artist JMW Turner landed on the Mewstone and made several sketches of the island.

Nearby places of interest:

Wembury Marine Centre *is based in Church Road, Wembury and allows visitors to learn about the surrounding area together with its wildlife. There are interactive displays as well as tanks and regular rockpool walks. Phone: 01752 862538.*

Thorn House and Garden at Wembury *sits on the banks of the River Yealm and offers the ideal venue for corporate events, as well as weddings and garden parties. The historical garden is opened by appointment. Phone: 01752 862494. E-mail: events@thornhouse.co.uk*

St Werburgh's Church *is situated above the beach at Wembury and looks out to the Yealm Estuary and the Mewstone. Much of the church was built in 1088, which replaced an earlier Saxon wooden building. Restoration took place in the 1880s.*

Wembury Bay Riding School is a family run livery yard which offers riding lessons throughout the year in an idyllic coastal setting. They have weekend children's clubs as well as a Tots' club and a Ladies' club. They open every day between 8:30am and 3pm. Tel: 01752 862676.

Heading back to the A379, the road leads to the small village of **Brixton** before reaching **Yealmpton.** The church at Brixton dates from the fifteenth century with a tower arch which is 200 years older. Views look towards the River Yealm.

At Yealmpton there is a 400-year-old stone cottage, where the nursery rhyme Old Mother Hubbard was supposedly written, and nearby are Kitley Caves where green marble was quarried. The British Museum contains an arch made of it. The conservative politician John Pollexfen Bastard (1756-1816), who was colonel of the East Devon Militia, once lived at Kitley House.

Taking a right turn on the road leads to the village of **Newton Ferrers**. It was mentioned in the Domesday book of 1086 where it was called Niwetone. A Norman family, Ferrers, were later given the village and it became Newton Ferrers. The notorious pirate, Henry Every, who lived in the seventeenth century, was born there.

The church of Holy Cross was re-built in 1260 before being enlarged in 1342 by the rector, Henry de Ferrers. It was later restored by George Fellowes Prynne in 1885 and the west tower and the north and south arcades remain from the original medieval building.

Across the creek from Newton Ferrers is **Noss Mayo**. The first recorded mention of the village is in 1286 when it was referred to as Nesse Matheu. The manor belonged to Matheu, son of John, between 1284 and 1309. The manor was given to Matthew Fitzjohn by Edward II in 1287.

The church in the village is dedicated to St Peter and was built in 1882. It was paid for by Edward Baring, the 1st Baron Revelstoke,

A vintage photo showing children playing on a boat on the tidal River Yealm, between the villages of Noss Mayo and Newton Ferrers.

who was the head of Barings Bank. An older church, dating from 1226, was on the coast, a mile to the south.

Heading back on the main road, a turn to the right leads to the village of **Holbeton** which once formed part of the Ermington Hundred. An Iron Age enclosure or hill fort, known as Holbury, can be found to the east of the village. The parish of Holbeton contains the historic estates of Flete, Mothecombe and Adeston.

Flete House is surrounded by a large park that was once the seat of Baron Mildmay of Flete. The house today has been converted into apartments. It was remodelled by architect Norman Shaw from

1878 onwards. He constructed the great tower on the north front and also rebuilt the north-west wing, as well as altering the interior.

Mothecombe has beautiful walks alongside a beach and estuary. The estate became the property of John Pollexfen (*circa* 1620) of Kitley who inherited it when he married the daughter and heiress of Stretchley of Mothecombe. In 1720 Mothecombe House was built by his great-great grandson John Pollexfen.

The remains of old kilns can be found on either side of the estuary as well as Second World War pillboxes.

There are two beaches, Mothecombe Beach (also known as Meadowsfoot Beach) and Coastguards Beach. The beaches have been used as the locations for many film and television programmes most notably *International Velvet* (1978), starring Tatum O'Neal, and *Hornblower* starring Ioan Gruffud.

Just off the A379 is the village of **Ermington** which dates back to Saxon times and was founded around the year 700AD. It is recorded as a royal manor in the Domesday Book. Nearby is Penquit which has been inhabited since the Celtic times of Dumnonia. Penquit in Celtic means 'end of the wood'. At Strashleigh is a thirteenth century mansion which originally belonged to the Strashleigh family and remained in their possession until 1583.

The market town of **Modbury** can be found on the A379 heading towards Kingsbridge. The Domesday Book mentions Modbury and the town was granted permission to hold a weekly fair some time before 1199. During the fourteenth century, the population of the town was greatly reduced due to the outbreak of the Black Death.

Two battles were fought there during the English Civil War. On 9 December 1642 the Royalists gained a victory when their soldiers fought off a small Parliamentarian force. The second battle took place on 21 February 1643 when the Royalists fortified the town in anticipation of an attack by Parliamentarian forces gathered at nearby Kingsbridge. The Royalists, outnumbered four to one and running out of ammunition, retreated. The victory was partly instrumental in the lifting of the siege of Plymouth, a Parliamentary stronghold which held out for four years against the king.

During the early nineteenth century the population of the market town had grown to 1,813. Many were involved in some way or another with the wool trade. Mechanisation of the wool industry led to a decline in population and economic prosperity as many workers left the area and headed to large cities to seek employment. Some travelled further afield with others emigrating to America. In the late 1800s many areas prospered because of the railway, but unfortunately it bypassed Modbury leading further to its decline. Modbury remained an important market town until 1944 when the cattle market came to an end.

Travelling from Modbury toward the coast, the village of **Ringmore** is discovered which was first mentioned in the Domesday book, which named it as 'Reimore'. There was a manor located there until 1908. From the small bay, many boats left to fish for pilchards and also to rescue sailors who found their vessels wrecked on the rocks at nearby Burgh Island.

From the village is a view of Bigbury Bay as well as Aymore Cove and there are two thirteenth-century buildings – the Church of All Hallows and The Journey's End Inn, which was previously known as The New Inn.

During the English Civil War the parish priest of All Hallows, William Lane, swore allegiance to King Charles I and turned against Cromwell. A band of Cromwell's men were sent from Plymouth by sea and landed at Aymer before heading to the rectory and burning it down. Two of William Lane's sons were taken prisoner, while Lane himself took refuge in a secret room in the tower of All Hallows. Parishioners looked after him for many weeks before he was able to escape to France. However, when he eventually returned to England, he was walking the route between London and Devon and drank water at the roadside which later led to him dying of fever, just

40 miles from home. He was buried under the communion table in the church at Alphington, close to Exeter.

The village of **Challaborough** beside the sea is very popular with surfers. It has two static caravan parks together with several houses. Most properties overlook Bigbury-on-Sea and Burgh Island. **Bigbury-on-Sea** can be reached by road or by walking the coastal path from Challaborough. At the beginning of the twentieth century, Bigbury-on-Sea included just a handful of fishermen's cottages together with fish cellars. Now the area is very popular with holidaymakers and has a beach café. Several films and television programmes have been

A view of the hotel on Burgh Island from the beach at Bigbury-on-Sea. Agatha Christie and Noël Coward once stayed there. The island was originally known as St Michael's Island. Its name later became Borough Island before being corrupted to Burgh Island.

The Pilchard Inn, dating from 1336, on Burgh Island. The inn is still open today and is very popular with locals and tourists.

shot here including *Holocaust 2000* (starring Kirk Douglas), *Dixon of Dock Green, Lovejoy* and Agatha Christie's *Evil Under the Sun*.

Burgh Island is joined to Bigbury-on-Sea by its sandy beach and it is possible to walk to the island during low tide. When the tide is in, a sea tractor takes visitors back and forth. Unusually, the tide comes in on both sides of the walkway.

The island has several notable buildings including the Art Deco Burgh Island Hotel, the Pilchard Inn (run by the hotel), a former chapel, as well as three private houses. It was important as a tin trading port during ancient times and tin ingots were discovered on the River Erme estuary wreck. The island is mentioned on early maps where it was called St Michael's Island. Its name later became Borough Island before being corrupted to Burgh Island. A monastery once existed there and it is thought that most of its remains lie beneath the hotel.

The Pilchard Inn may, at one time, have included guest lodgings for the monastery. Fishermen occupied the island following the dissolution of the monastery and were greatly involved in the pilchard trade.

The remains of an ancient chapel can be found on top of the island. It later became a 'huers hut' where fishermen made a hue and cry call to each other revealing the location of shoals of pilchards. During this time, smuggling, wrecking and piracy also took place.

During the 1890s George H. Chirgwin, a music hall star, built a wooden house on the island which was used by his guests during weekend parties. In 1927 the island was sold to filmmaker, Archibald Nettlefold, of Nettlefold Studios. He was the heir to the Guest, Keen and Nettlefolds engineering firm, and together they built a more substantial Art Deco style hotel. It became a popular destination for the rich and famous during the 1930s. During the same decade, a room was created from the captain's cabin of the warship, HMS *Ganges*.

The hotel became a recovery centre for injured RAF personnel during the Second World War and was damaged by enemy bombing. Fears of a German invasion led to the area being fortified with anti-tank defences and two pillboxes.

Agatha Christie visited the island and stayed at the hotel which served as the setting for *Soldier Island (And Then There Were None)* as well as the setting of the Hercule Poirot mystery, *Evil Under the Sun*. Noël Coward also stayed there.

The end scene of the 1965 movie *Catch Us If You Can*, starring The Dave Clark Five, took place on the island. The Beatles also stayed at the hotel while appearing in Plymouth. Other notable guests included Edward and Mrs Simpson as well as Eisenhower and Churchill who met there in the weeks leading up to D-Day.

CHAPTER 5

Bantham to Kingsbridge

Bantham is a small coastal village in the South Hams district beside the estuary of the River Avon.

Records show that Bantham was once a port selling tin to the Gauls during Roman times. A large settlement was built by the Romans which lay behind the dunes close to the current village with the purpose of protecting the entrance of the river at Bantham Ham. The

The small boathouse at Bantham which lies beside the estuary of the River Avon. During Roman times, Bantham was a port which made a living selling tin to the Gauls.

An older photo showing the quiet main village street at Thurlestone. The village is named after Thurlestone Rock, an arch-shaped rock formation found nearby at Thurlestone Bay.

settlement existed into post-Roman Britain and was later covered by sand. In the mid 1700s a storm uncovered the burnt remains of the settlement. When landowners drained the nearby marshes in the 1800s, they discovered human bones which they took away and sold.

Between 1750 and 1880 Bantham was the centre of the regional pilchard trade. Vast quantities of pilchards were processed in Cornwall before being dispatched to France and Spain, sold locally or traded with Italy. The trade eventually declined due to over fishing and the village saw its fortunes disappear.

Further along the coast from Bantham, and 5 miles from Kingbridge, is **Thurlestone**, a small seaside village with a population of approximately 1,886. The village is named after Thurlestone Rock, an arch-shaped rock formation found nearby at Thurlestone Bay. All Saints Church in the village dates from the thirteenth century and was added to in the fifteenth and sixteenth centuries.

Hope Cove is a small coastal village in the South Hams District, 5 miles west of Salcombe. The village has two beaches and is

A view looking towards Salcombe. A Bronze Age shipwreck lies off the coast of Salcombe and once contained jewellery and weapons from France.

sheltered by Bolt Tail, the nearby headland. The Spanish Armada was spotted passing by the village in 1588 as its ships sailed up the English Channel. When the Armada was defeated and was heading back through storms, one of its ships, the *San Pedro el Mayor*, blew on to the rocks between Inner and Outer Hope. All 140 survivors, who were taken captive, were originally sentenced to death but were later ransomed before being sent home to Spain.

The Victorian artist Sir Luke Fildes painted a number of studies there, the most famous being the cottage in his work, 'The Doctor'.

Salcombe has an extensive waterfront and is particularly popular with people interested in sailing, yachting and other types of water sports. Properties tend to be very expensive in the area. The town falls within the South Devon Area of Outstanding Natural Beauty (AONB) and is home to a traditional shellfish fishing industry.

A Bronze Age shipwreck lies off the coast of Salcombe and contained jewellery and weapons from France. A seventeenth-century shipwreck was found to contain 400 Moroccan gold coins and items from Holland.

During 1936 the *Herzogin Cecilie*, a four-masted barque from Finland, ran aground near the Ham Stone. It was later beached at Starehole Bay, close to Bolt Head. In 1957 HMS *Untiring*, a U-Class submarine from the Second World War, was sunk off Salcombe to be used as a sonar target.

In 1244 Salcombe first appeared in the records marked as being on the boundary of Batson and West Portlemouth. The town was mentioned in 1570 when it was said that there were fifty-six mariners operating from there. A survey two years later said that five ships under 60 tons were moored at Salcombe. In 1566 it was recorded that there were ten seine nets at Salcombe. In the 1580s fishermen from Salcombe travelled annually to Padstow in connection with the new herring fishery where they rented cottages and storehouses.

In the English Civil War of the seventeenth century Salcombe pledged allegiance to the king and held out against the Parliamentarians. Towards the south of the town can be found the remains of Fort Charles, which was held from January to May 1646 and was the last Royalist stronghold. Henry VIII originally built the fort to defend the estuary. It was later slighted (destroyed) on the orders of Parliament.

During the late seventeenth and early eighteenth centuries, local people relied on fishing and smuggling for their income. By the nineteenth century the town had become a major port for shipping in the fruit trade. Ships left Salcombe and sailed to Iberia, the Mediterranean and the Caribbean, together with the Azores and Newfoundland. The main fruit cargoes consisted of oranges and lemons from the Azores, as well as pineapples from the Bahamas and West Indies. Other loads brought to the port included sugar, rum, coconuts and shaddocks. Wood such as ebony and mahogany was also carried for furnishing ships. Both Salcombe and Kingsbridge became popular ship-building towns and produced the Salcombe schooner, a fast boat that required fewer hands to sail it.

The Salcombe fleet carried coal from Wales as well as cider, malt, grain and slates.

In 1870 there was a ferry to Brest from Salcombe but it was short-lived. By 1871 there were 776 people living in the main part of the town. These included thirty-four shipwrights together with thirteen ship's carpenters, five sawyers, three block makers, two ship's riggers, three sail makers, a tin plate worker and four blacksmiths.

The fruit trade declined in the 1870s due to diseases that affected oranges and pineapples. Another cause of the decline was the advent of steamships. There was a limited amount of work for local vessels carrying salt to Newfoundland and returning with cod. By 1914 only three or four locally owned trading ships remained in the estuary.

However, pleasure sailing became popular and in 1874 the yacht club was founded. In 1864, Salcombe had become a ship registry port and came under Dartmouth for customs. A customs house was eventually built at Salcombe and still exists today.

As many as 200 vessels were launched at Salcombe between 1796 and 1887. Shipyards were built on reclaimed foreshore with new shipyards at Shadycombe Creek. Many vessels were lost at sea, including seven boats off the Azores during November 1851. Many of the Victorian houses in Salcombe today were built by shipowners and masters. With the arrival of larger ships and steam propulsion after 1880, fewer new vessels were built at Salcombe and less repair work was carried out. Many men in the town found work in the dockyards or at deep sea fishing ports.

In 1824 a turnpike was built to Salcombe which was originally part of the Malborough parish. A chapel-of-ease had previously been built at Salcombe in 1401, although the parish church was not constructed until the nineteenth century.

Between the First and Second World Wars, the town was developed as a holiday resort and the Salcombe Sailing Club was founded in 1922.

Salcombe became an Advance Amphibious Base for the United States Navy during the Second World War. A radar station was set up on Bolt Head in September 1943. The Navy's headquarters were at the Salcombe Hotel and a further sixty properties were requisitioned. Quonset huts were constructed on the hill near the Rugby Club. At the same time, the building of Whitestrand Quay and the slipway took place. A total of 137 officers and 1,793 men were based at Salcombe. On 4 June 1944 in preparation for D-Day two days later, sixty-six ships and many auxiliary vessels left from Salcombe as part of Force U which later landed on Utah Beach, Normandy.

The shipyards at Shadycombe Creek and Mill Bay were later used to repair damaged landing craft before the base shut on 7 May 1945. The area suffered several bombing raids during the war and many civilians were killed.

During the Cold War, the radar station at Bolt Head was used as the Regional Seat of Government in the event of an enemy attack. It was later dismantled.

Nearby places of interest:
Overbecks Museum and Garden *is a National Trust property on cliffs above Salcombe. It includes a museum, tea garden and subtropical gardens. It was originally the seaside home of the inventor, Otto Overbeck. Phone: 01548 842893.*

Bolberry Down *is an easy to access clifftop walk owned by the National Trust. The walk takes you to Overbecks and Salcombe to the east or to Hope Cove and South Milton Sands to the west. The remains of an Iron Age fort can be found at Bolt Tail.*

The Salcombe Distilling Company *is located at 28 Island Street and produces Salcombe Gin and also allows the visitor to make their own gin as well as sample the produce. Phone: 01548 288180. Email: ilovegin@salcombedistilling.com*

Salcombe Maritime Museum includes a vast collection of models, paintings, photographs and memorabilia relating to Salcombe's links with the sea. It is located in Market Street and opens between April and October. Phone: 01548 843 080 (opening hours only). Email: info@salcombemuseum.org.uk

Situated at the southern end of the Kingsbridge Estuary, **East Portlemouth** is a small village with an approximate population of 160. It has a popular beach and a ferry that runs to Salcombe. The village was first mentioned in the Domesday book of 1086 when it was called Porlamuta which means 'mouth of the port well'. Portlemouth features many second homes for celebrities such as Steve Rider, Michael Parkinson and Kate Bush.

East Prawle is a small village which lies within the Chivelstone parish of the South Hams. It is situated close to the coast, south-east of Salcombe. The village is mentioned in the Domesday Book and its name comes from the Anglo Saxon word Præwhyll which means 'lookout place'. East Prawle mainly draws its income from farming but the village also has a pub, a local shop and a community hall. An airfield was built outside the village during the First World War. There is one public house in the village with the unusual name, The Pig's Nose. It is well-known for hosting live music events and artists who have appeared there include Wishbone Ash, the Animals, the Yardbirds, Atomic Kitten and the Boomtown Rats.

Start Point is well-known for its lighthouse which was built due to the many shipwrecks in the area. Erected in 1836, the lighthouse warned sailors of the danger of the point and nearby rocks. It is a popular tourist attraction with people visiting for the stunning views and the variety of birdlife.

A chapel has existed in **Hallsands** since 1506, although it is thought that the village was not inhabited before 1600. During the eighteenth and nineteenth centuries the village grew and in 1891

The lighthouse at Start Point. The word 'Start' comes from the Anglo-Saxon word steort, meaning a tail. The lighthouse was constructed in 1836 after countless shipping disasters.

The village of Hallsands shown in 1885 before it was destroyed by storms.

The beach leading to Hallsands. During January 1917 high tides and strong gales breached Hallsands' defences destroying the village and leaving only one house habitable.

it had a population of 159, together with 37 houses, a spring and a public house, the London Inn. The main source of income at the time came from fishing, including crab fishing at nearby Skerries Bank.

When the naval dockyard was expanded at Keyham in Devonport in the 1890s, dredging took place off the shores of Hallsands and removed sand and gravel to be used in the construction process. This led to 1,600 tons of material being removed each day and the beach level dropped alarmingly. Concerns were raised by the villagers who felt that the dredging was undermining the area and threatening the village. An inquiry stated that the removal caused no harm and the process continued.

In the autumn storms of 1900 part of the sea wall was washed away and in November villagers petitioned their MP complaining that the work was causing damage to their houses. By March 1901 Kingsbridge Rural District Council had written to the Board of Trade and complained about the damage to the road. In September 1901 an inspector from the Board of Trade decided that dredging should stop as further severe storms could cause serious damage to the area. The dredging licence

A photo showing Hallsands after it had been destroyed by storms. Mrs Elizabeth Prettejohn was reported to be the last inhabitant of the village in 1960.

was revoked on 8 January 1902. The level of the beach recovered during 1902 but the winter of that year brought more storms and damage.

During January 1917 high tides and strong gales breached Hallsands' defences, destroying the village and leaving only one house habitable. In 1960 it was reported that the last inhabitant of the village was Mrs Elizabeth Prettejohn.

The village of **Beesands** is located between Hallsands and Torcross on the coast of Start Bay. Its income comes from fishing as well as the tourist trade. There is an Anglican church, dedicated to St Andrew, in the village. Beesands Ley, a freshwater lake, lies behind the beach to the north of the village.

The name Beesands comes from 'Bay Sands' and the area was first inhabited during the late 1700s after the threat of seaward pirates had diminished. In 1805 there were just six dwellings there but by 1841 there were 104 people living in seventeen houses, the majority of whom were supported by the fishing trade. The King's Arms became the first public house and was opened in 1823. It closed in 1910.

Keith Richards, later of the Rolling Stones, visited Beesands with his family during the 1950s. Together with Mick Jagger, he gave his first public performance at The Cricket Inn within the village.

Looking along the beach at Beesands. The name Beesands comes from 'Bay Sands' and the area was first inhabited during the late 1700s after the threat of seaward pirates had diminished.

Torcross lies at the southern end of Slapton Sands. The sands separate Slapton Ley, a freshwater lake, from Start Bay. The village was first mentioned in records in 1602. The coastal road linking Kingsbridge and Dartmouth was built in 1854 and passed through Torcross, providing a lifeline to the community. A coach service started between Dartmouth and Kingsbridge in 1858. The village originally drew its income from farming and fishing, but in the late 1800s many tourists visited the area, which, at the time, had three hotels and ten B&Bs.

Torcross and nearby villages were evacuated during 1943 in readiness for the D-Day landings. Approximately 15,000 allied troops were stationed in the area. Tragedy occurred on 28 April 1944 when, during a live-firing rehearsal for D-Day (Exercise Tiger), nine German torpedo boats attacked a convoy of vessels travelling between Portland and Slapton Sands which were taking part in the exercise. Two tank landing vessels were sunk, one badly damaged

The view from Torcross looking towards Slapton Sands. The village was first mentioned in records in 1602 and the coastal road linking Kingsbridge and Dartmouth was built in 1854.

D-Day rehearsals taking place at Torcross during the Second World War. Approximately 15,000 allied troops were stationed in the area at the time.

A Sherman tank at Torcross which serves as a memorial for the men who lost their lives during the Second World War.

and 946 American servicemen lost their lives. Communication problems and the absence of a Royal Navy ship undergoing repairs, together with incorrectly worn life jackets, contributed to the loss of life. In all over 1,000 men died during the operation and an unknown number were injured, many due to friendly fire on the beach. A complete blackout was put on the incident and survivors were sworn to secrecy on pain of court martial.

Today, a Sherman amphibious tank stands at Torcross car park between Slapton Ley and the beach as a memorial to all the men who lost their lives there. The finance to salvage the tank from the waters of Start Bay came from the late Ken Small, a hotelier in Torcross. The salvage operation was completed in 1984. Several plaques also commemorate the event.

The picturesque pebble beach at Slapton. Slapton Sands was first mentioned in the Domesday book when it was known as Sladone.

Thatched cottages at Strete. The village lies on an ancient trackway and the name Strete comes from the Old English word, Strǣt, meaning a road or a Roman road.

Holidaymakers at Blackpool Sands. Today, the area is a popular tourist destination surrounded by evergreens and tall pines.

Slapton Sands was mentioned in the Domesday book as Sladone. In 1372 Sir Guy de Brian founded the Collegiate Chantry of St Mary. The Tower Inn and West tower still stand and in recent years, English Heritage has listed the tower as a Grade I listed building. The Church of St James was built in the late thirteenth century and is also grade I listed. The beach, which is a coastal bar, is made up of small pebbles.

Strete is a small village on the A379 between Kingsbridge and Dartmouth which lies behind Pilchard Cove at the north end of Slapton Sands. Until 1836 a medieval church stood in the village. It was replaced by a church dedicated to St Michael. The area was first referred to in 1194 when it was called Streta. By 1244 it was being called Strete which comes from the Old English word, Strǣt, meaning a road or a Roman road. On maps until the late 1800s, the village was referred to as 'Street'.

Nearby **Blackpool Sands** is a popular tourist destination with a sheltered bay surrounded by pines and evergreens. There are cafés and a shop where kayaks, rafts and paddleboards can be hired.

A vintage photo showing the main car-lined street in Kingsbridge. Many eighteenth and nineteenth century buildings still stand in the town, including the Shambles.

Stoke Fleming is recorded in the Domesday Book as Stoc. The name 'le Flemeng' was attached to the village's name in approximately 1218 and this later became Stoke Fleming. The thirteenth century parish church is dedicated to St Peter and was enlarged in the fourteenth century. A major restoration took place between 1871 and 1872. Earmund of Stoke Fleming, an Anglo-Saxon saint, is buried there. Also buried in the graveyard is George Parker Bidder (1806-1878), better known as 'the Calculating Boy'.

Kingsbridge is a market town with a population of approximately 6,120. A bridge dating from the tenth century gave its name to the settlement lying between the royal estates of Alvington and Chillington leading to the name 'Kyngysbrygge' meaning 'King's bridge'. The Abbot of Buckfast was granted the right to hold a market in the town in 1219 and this led to Kingsbridge becoming a borough in 1238. The manor belonged to the abbot until the Dissolution of the Monasteries when it was gifted to Sir William Petre.

Kingsbridge originally combined two towns: Kingsbridge and Dodbrooke. Dodbrooke was granted its own market in 1257 before

The quay at Kingsbridge together with the war memorial containing the names of local residents who lost their lives during the First World War.

becoming a borough in 1319. Two ecclesiastical parishes lie within Kingsbridge, St Edmund's in the west and St Thomas Becket at Dodbrooke in the east. St Edmunds was built in the 1200s and retains some of its features from that time, including its font. However, it was enlarged in 1414 and largely rebuilt in the 1800s. A well-preserved rood screen is displayed in the parish church of St Thomas Becket which was restored in 1897.

The local mills were converted to produce wool in 1798 and large quantities of cloth were made. Also during the 1800s, the town's industries included a tannery, a coastal shipping trade and a large monthly cattle market. Exports included corn, malt, slate and cider.

Many eighteenth and nineteenth century buildings still stand in the town including the Shambles, the market arcade, which was rebuilt in 1796. Its sixteenth century granite piers are incorporated into the building. Thomas Crispin built the former grammar school in 1670 which today is a museum. William Cookworthy, the chemist, was

Fore Street in Kingsbridge. The town's name was originally 'Kyngysbrygge' meaning 'King's bridge, which was named after a bridge dating from the tenth century which lay between the royal estates of Alvington and Chillington.

The cliff railway at Babbacombe. The railway has shuttled holidaymakers to and from Oddicombe beach since 1926 and allows visitors to take in the wonderful surrounding scenery.

born in Kingsbridge in 1705 and a museum recognises his work. He found china clay in Cornwall and developed a way to process it into porcelain items.

The town lies on the A379 road which links to Plymouth and Dartmouth. Salcombe and Totnes are linked to the town by the A381.

The railway station at Kingsbridge was closed in 1963 after welcoming passengers for seventy years. The branch line which ran via South Brent was discontinued and led to the closure of the station at Kingsbridge. The removal was due to the Beeching cuts which affected many railways services all over the country.

Nearby places of interest:
Babbacombe Model Village *is one of Torquay's main tourist attractions and is located at Hampton Avenue, Babbacombe. It opens between 1st May and 23rd July from 10am to 4pm, except on Thursdays for illuminations when it opens between 10am and 9pm. Phone: 01803 315315. Email: mail@model-village.co.uk*

Fast Rabbit Garden *covers an area of 42 acres in the secluded Strawberry Valley in Dartmouth. It includes beautiful gardens, scenery, wildlife as well as a plant sale centre. Phone: 07813 504490. Email: catchall@fastrabbitfarm.co.uk*

The Kingsbridge and District Light Railway *runs small trains for mainly children but also adults, alongside the Kingsbridge estuary. Phone: 07885 227000*

Harbour House *is a centre for arts and yoga and includes a gallery and vegetarian café. It is located at the Promenade in Kingsbridge. Phone: 01548 854708. Email: info@harbourhouse.org.uk*

CHAPTER 6

Dartmouth to Totnes

Dartmouth is a town on the western side of the River Dart. The deep-water port has proved vitally important to sailing vessels. In 1147, and again in 1190, the port was the starting point for the Second and Third Crusades. Warfleet Creek, which is close to Dartmouth Castle, was supposedly named after the vast flee of ships which at one time assembled there.

Dartmouth Castle has guarded the entrance to the estuary for over 600 years and saw action during the civil war.

The view from Bayard's Fort, a Tudor artillery fort, which was built between 1522 and 1536 and once contained heavy guns to protect Dartmouth harbour.

Since the reign of Edward II, Dartmouth has been a home to the Royal Navy. During the Hundred Years War the town was twice attacked. After these events the harbour was closed each evening by a large chain to repel intruders. Two castles guard the entrance to the narrow mouth of the Dart: Dartmouth Castle and Kingswear Castle.

The town was visited by Geoffrey Chaucer who wrote about it in his Canterbury Tales. In medieval times Dartmouth was involved in privateering and the mayor, John Hawley, himself a privateer, was the model for Chaucer's 'schipman'.

Smith Street is the oldest recorded street name in Dartmouth, appearing in records in the thirteenth century. Some buildings date from the late sixteenth and early seventeenth centuries and were built on the site of earlier medieval houses. Smith Street gets its name from the many smiths and shipwrights who once repaired ships in the area. The town pillory was also located at Smith Street during medieval times.

In 1335 St Saviour's Church was built and was consecrated in 1372. Inside is the tomb of John Hawley, who died in 1408, together with those of his two wives. A pre-Reformation oak rood screen was constructed in 1480 and also stands within the church.

A Portuguese treasure ship, the *Madre de Deus*, was taken by the English in the Azores in 1592. It was later brought to Dartmouth Harbour. The vessel was met by traders, dealers, cutpurses and thieves stripping the vessel of much that was of value. When Sir Walter Raleigh arrived to claim the Crown's share of the prize, the cargo had been reduced in value from £500,000 to £140,000. Ten freighters were employed to carry the remaining treasure back to London.

When Henry Hudson landed at Dartmouth after returning from North America, he was immediately arrested for displaying a foreign flag. On the way from Southampton to America, the Pilgrim Fathers moored at Bayard Cove, taking rest, before continuing their journey on the *Mayflower* and the *Speedwell* on 20 August 1620. The *Speedwell* proved to be unseaworthy and 300 miles west of

Smith Street in Dartmouth is the oldest recorded street name in the town, first appearing in records in the thirteenth century. The town pillory was located at Smith Street during medieval times.

A fine example of a Tudor building in Dartmouth which today houses Skippers restaurant.

Land's End, it sailed back to Plymouth. The *Mayflower* completed the crossing on its own, landing at Cape Cod.

Dartmouth features many medieval and Elizabethan buildings which are listed. The Butterwalk, built between 1635 and 1640, has a carved wooden fascia supported on granite columns. In 1671 Charles II held court in the Butterwalk while sheltering from a storm. The room is now part of Dartmouth museum with much of the interior still surviving. In 1639 the Royal Castle Hotel was built on the quay. Its new frontage was built in the 1800s while the original lies beneath. The oldest building in the town is an old merchant's house in Higher Street which was built in 1380. Today it houses the public house, The Cherub. Agincourt House, close to the Lower Ferry, also dates from the 1300s.

When the English fleet attacked the Spanish Armada, many of the ships came from Dartmouth. These included the *Roebuck,*

Crescent and *Hart*. The Spanish Armada's payship, the *Nuestra Señora del Rosario*, which was commanded by Admiral Pedro de Valdés, was captured by Sir Francis Drake and moored in the River Dart for more than a year. The crew were forced to work as labourers on the nearby Greenway Estate. At the time, it was the home of Sir Humphrey Gilbert and his half-brother Sir Walter Raleigh. Greenway later became the home of the author, Dame Agatha Christie.

At Gallants Bower are the remains of a civil war defensive structure. In 1643 the Royalist forces constructed the fort which lies to the south-east of the town. There is a similar fort at Mount Ridley on the opposite slope at Kingswear. In 1646 General Thomas Fairfax, Parliamentary commander-in-chief, led an attack from the north which resulted in the town being captured and the Royalists surrendering. Soon after, Gallants Bower was demolished.

In the 1800s land was reclaimed and the embankment was formed which stretches the length of the riverbank. The work was carried out by Napoleonic prisoners, of which there were many captive in the town. Previously, the area now covered by the town centre was mainly made up of tidal mud flats.

In 1878 the Dart Lifeboat Station was opened by the Royal National Lifeboat Institution at Sand Quay, but closed in 1896.

The Britannia Royal Naval College was completed in 1905. Naval officers have been trained at Dartmouth since 1863 when the wooden hulk of HMS *Britannia* moored in the River Dart was used as a base. In 1864, *Britannia* was supplemented by HMS *Hindostan*. Before this the Royal Naval Academy (later the Royal Naval College) had been based for more than a hundred years between 1733 and 1837 at Portsmouth. In 1869, the original *Britannia* was replaced by the *Prince of Wales* and was renamed *Britannia*. King Edward VII laid the foundation stone for a new building at the college in March 1902. The shore-based college was designed by Sir Aston Webb and was built by Higgs and Hill.

During the Second World War Dartmouth became one of the departure points on the south coast for American troops heading for

Utah Beach as part of the D-Day landings. Much of the surrounding area was closed to the public, including the countryside and nearby Slapton Sands, while the American forces rehearsed for the Normandy landings.

The town has had many famous residents including Thomas Newcomen who invented the atmospheric engine, the first successful steam-powered pumping engine. Newcomen was born in Dartmouth in 1663 and lived in the vicinity of Lower Street, which today is marked with a plaque. The original building was in the 1800s and replaced with a new road which was named after Newcomen. A working Newcomen steam engine from the 1700s is displayed in Dartmouth.

George Parker Bidder (1806-1878), the calculating prodigy and civil engineer, also lived in the town. He worked on railways all over the world as well as carrying out work on the docks in the East End of London. He served on the town council and his skill was called upon when the area, which is now the centre of the town, was drained. Joining forces with Samuel Lake, he carried out pioneering work on steam trawling whilst living locally. His home was at Paradise Point, near Warfleet where he died in 1878. He is buried at Stoke Fleming.

Another famous resident was Flora Thompson whose home between 1928 and 1940 was in Above Town. During the time she lived in the area, she wrote *Lark Rise* and *Over to Candleford* which were later combined into a single volume and published as *Lark Rise to Candleford*. She is buried at Longcross Cemetery.

Rachel Kempson, the stage and film actress, was born in Dartmouth in 1910. She later became the wife of Sir Michael Redgrave and mother to Vanessa, Lynn and Corin. Her autobiography, *Life Among the Redgraves*, was published in 1988. She died in 2003.

Well-known people who attended the Royal Naval College included Gordon Onslow Ford (1912-2003), the British surrealist painter and Sir John Harvey Jones (1924-2008), a businessman and television presenter. Christopher Robin Milne once owned the Harbour

Bookshop in Dartmouth. He was the son of A.A. Milne, and the character, Christopher Robin, in the Winnie-the-Pooh books was named after him.

Dartmouth has been used in many television productions, most famously Bayard's Cove which was seen in the 1970s seafaring drama, *The Onedin Line.*

The BBC's *Down to Earth* (2000), starring Ricky Tomlinson, was also filmed at Dartmouth as was *The Coroner* (2015-2016) starring Claire Goose.

Nearby places of interest:

Coleton Fishacre *is a National Trust property located at Brownstone Road, Kingswear, set in 24 acres, which includes a garden and house decorated in an Art Deco fashion. The garden heads towards the sea at Pudcombe Cove. Phone: 01803 842382.*

Greenway *is located at Galmpton near Brixham. It was once the holiday home of Agatha Christie. Today, it belongs to the National Trust and the house and gardens are open to the public. The inside of the house is decorated in a 1950s style and is how it would have looked when Agatha Christie stayed there.*

The Britannia Royal Naval College *at Dartmouth is the initial officer training establishment of the Royal Navy. Tours take place throughout the year, generally on Monday afternoons as well as Wednesday afternoons in the high season. Phone: 01803 677565 or email: tours@britanniaassociation.org.uk*

Blackpool Sands *is a scenic sheltered beach surrounded by evergreens and pines located 3 miles west of Dartmouth. Lifeguards patrol the beach during the summer months and there is a café and shop which allows visitors to hire stand-up paddle boards, kayaks and wet suits. Phone: 01803 771800.*

Dartmouth Castle *is located at the entrance of the Dart Estuary and is open between 1 April and 30 September. The earliest parts of the castle date from the 1380s. As well as exhibits and events, there is a shop and café offering cream teas. Phone: 01803 833588 or 839618.*

Woodlands Family Theme Park *is an amusement park located 5 miles from Dartmouth. It is the largest family theme park in Devon and attracts thousands of visitors each year. It opens daily between 9.30am and 5pm. A camping site can be found nearby. Phone: 01803 712598. Email: fun@woodlandspark.com*

Dartmouth Museum *is located at The Butterwalk, Duke Street in Dartmouth. It includes an extensive display of artefacts, models, paintings and photographs concerning Dartmouth and the surrounding area. Phone: 01803 832923. Email: dartmouth@ devonmuseums.net*

Manor Street at Dittisham-on-the-Dart. Dittisham is approximately 2 miles upstream from Dartmouth and a ferry runs from the village to Greenway Quay, close to the Greenway Estate which was once the home of Agatha Christie.

Dittisham can be found on the banks of the River Dart, approximately 2 miles upstream from Dartmouth. A ferry runs from the village to Greenway Quay which lies beside the Greenway Estate, once the home to Agatha Christie. Today, the estate is owned by the National Trust.

Stoke Gabriel lies further up the River Dart towards Totnes. An Iron Age Fort existed at Portbridge in about 500BC and was inhabited until the sixth century. It was farmed by a small Celtic community. The Saxons took over when the Danes raided communities on the River Dart.

The earliest record of the village appears in the Domesday Book of 1073 which mentions a church at Stoke Gabriel. The village was inhabited by fishermen and farm workers and orchards were planted to supply them with cider. The Church House Inn in the village dates back to 1152.

An old photo showing Mill View at Stoke Gabriel. A 1,000-year-old yew tree stands in the churchyard of The Church of St Mary and St Gabriel. The church dates back to Norman times.

For centuries Stoke Gabriel was the centre of the Dart salmon industry but fish stocks diminished greatly over the years. At one time a ferry linked the west of the South Hams with Stoke Gabriel from Duncannon to Ashprington Point but it came to a halt at the start of the Second World War.

Famous residents have included John Davis, who was born at Sandridge, a sailor and explorer as well as a friend of Sir Walter Raleigh. He invented the quadrant and discovered the passage between Greenland and Baffin Island, now named the Davis Strait. In 1592 he discovered the Falkland Islands; he was killed by pirates in 1605.

George Jackson Churchward was born at Rowes Farm on Aish Road in 1857. He found fame as a steam locomotive designer and revolutionised boiler design in steam engines. He retired in 1922 and died in 1933 after tragically being hit by a steam locomotive close to the Swindon Works.

Further along the River Dart, towards Totnes, lies **Bowden House** which falls in the parish of Ashprington. The manor house was built in 1509 for John Gyles and was remodelled for Nicholas Trist between 1700 and 1704, with new south-east and south-west fronts.

The market town of **Totnes** lies at the head of the estuary of the River Dart. Its history dates back to 907AD when a castle was built there. By the twelfth century it was an important market town. Many merchants' houses were built within the town during the sixteenth and seventeenth centuries. The name Totnes derives from the Old English name 'Totta' and 'ness', meaning headland.

In 1136 Geoffrey of Monmouth wrote in his *Historia Regum Britanniae* that the coast of Totnes was where Brutus of Troy, the mythical founder of Britain, first set foot on the island. A small granite boulder, known as the 'Brutus Stone' is set into the pavement in Fore Street. It is said to mark the spot where Brutus first stepped from his ship. At the time, he is said to have declared: 'Here I stand and here I rest. And this town shall be called Totnes.' The stone lies far above where the highest tide settled and the stone isn't mentioned until 1697 when it is recorded in John Prince's *Worthies of Devon*. The stone may actually mark the location where the town crier, or bruiter, called his bruit or news. It's also possible that it may be le Brodestone, a boundary stone mentioned in several fifteenth century disputes. The last-known location of le Brodestone was in 1471 when it was below the East Gate.

The first authenticated recording of Totnes comes in 907AD, when the town was fortified by King Edward the Elder forming part of a defensive ring of burhs (old English fortifications) which were built around Devon. These replaced one built previously at nearby Halwell. The site lay on an ancient trackway which at low tide forded the river.

By 1523 Totnes had become the second richest town in Devon, and the sixteenth richest in England. King Edward VI granted Totnes a charter which allowed the former Benedictine priory building to

A vintage photo showing the Butterwalk at Totnes. The history of the town dates back to AD 907 when a castle was built there. By the twelfth century, it was an important market town.

be used as Totnes Guildhall and a school. By 1624 the Guildhall had been converted into a magistrate's court. During the English Civil War, troops were billeted there. In 1646 Oliver Cromwell visited Totnes for discussions with the general and parliamentary commander-in-chief, Thomas Fairfax, who was the 3rd Lord Fairfax of Cameron.

Until 1887 the Guildhall was used as the town prison and remained a magistrate's court until 1974.

Nearby places of interest:

Totnes Museum *is located at 70 Fore Street and is housed within an Elizabethan merchant's house which was originally built in 1575. There are twelve galleries as well as a courtyard and a herb garden. The exhibits date from 5000BC onwards and include coins minted in Totnes during Saxon times. Phone: 01803 863821. E-mail: info@ totnesmuseum.org*

Totnes Guildhall *is open to visitors between Monday and Friday from 11am to 3pm from 8 May until the end of September (excluding Bank Holidays). On Saturdays, the opening times are between 10am and 4pm. It is located at 5 Ramparts Walk in Totnes. The original priory building dates back to 1088 and there is much to explore within it. Phone: 01803 862147. Email: mayor@totnestowncouncil.gov.uk*

Totnes Castle *is owned by English Heritage and is a classic Norman motte and bailey castle. From the top, there are magnificent views over Totnes and towards the River Dart. It is open daily between 10am and 6pm and is located at Castle Street. Phone: 0370 333 1181.*

CHAPTER 7

Brixham to Torquay

The small fishing town of **Brixham** lies at the southern end of Torquay and today, tourism and fishing are its main source of income. The town's name was originally Brioc's village. 'Brioc' being an old English name added to 'ham' which was an ancient term for 'home'.

The hilly town has built up around the harbour. A tourist attraction is a replica of Sir Francis Drake's ship, the *Golden Hind*.

Brixham harbour with Brixham Hill in the background. Trading took place in the area during the Bronze Age and the first record of the town appears during Saxon times.

The replica of the Golden Hind *moored at Brixham harbour. The ship has been moored in the harbour since 1963 after it was used in the television series* Sir Francis Drake. *Today, it is a major tourist attraction.*

During the summer the Cowtown Carnival takes place every year in July at St Mary's Park. Originally, Brixham was two separate communities connected by a marshy lane. At the top of the hill was Cowtown, where the farmers lived, and at the bottom, the harbour, was Fishtown, where the fishermen and other sea dwellers lived. Cowtown can be found on the south-west road leaving Brixham heading towards Kingswear.

Brixham harbour was thought to have been inhabited during the Ice Age and trading took place there during the Bronze Age. The first record of the town appears in Saxon times and it is thought that a Saxon settlement originated from the sea in the sixth century or overland in the ninth century. In the Domesday Book the town was known as Briseham and the population was just thirty-nine. The town's value in 1334 was recorded as one pound, twelve shillings and eight pence. Its value increased to twenty-four pounds and sixteen shillings in 1524.

During the Middle Ages Brixham had the largest fishing port in the south-west of England and its fishing boats contributed to establishing the fishing industries of Hull, Grimsby and Lowestoft.

In 1350 William de Whithurst, an official of the Crown as well as a judge in Ireland, was appointed the parish priest of Brixham. The town is recorded as a borough from 1536 and a market was held there from 1822.

On 5 November 1688, William, Prince of Orange landed at Brixham harbour with his Dutch army before becoming King William III of Great Britain and Ireland. On landing, he proclaimed, 'The liberties of England and the Protestant religion I will maintain.'

His army made their camp at Overgang which is Dutch for 'passing' or 'crossing'. Many local people today have Dutch surnames and are descended from the soldiers who landed with William.

In 1801 the population of the town was 3,671 which grew to 8,092 in 1901.

The composer of the hymn *Abide With Me*, the Reverend Francis Lyte, was the vicar at All Saints Church which was founded in 1815. His home was at Berry Head House which today is a hotel. St Mary's Church is located a mile from the sea and is the town's main church. It is the third church to have been built on the site, which was originally an ancient burial ground. A wooden Saxon church was replaced by a stone one in Norman times and this was replaced in 1360.

Many of the cottages in the town were once home to the fishermen who worked in the area. In 1868 Brixham was linked to the railway and carried passengers and local produce, mostly fish. The line closed in 1963 due to the Beeching cuts.

Berry Head is a coastal headland lying to the south-east of Brixham. Originally, an Iron Age hill fort was on the site but most of this was destroyed when extensive fortifications were built in the area between

The fortifications at Berry Head. The area was fortified between 1794 and 1804 to protect Torbay from invading French armies.

1794 and 1804 to protect Torbay from the threat of invading French armies. The former artillery house contains information about the fortification and a history of the area.

Berry Head also has an abundance of bird life including guillemots, razorbills and black-legged kittiwakes.

The Board of Ordnance originally built the nearby hospital as a military one to serve the three Napoleonic war forts at Berry Head. Afterwards, it became the home of hymnist and poet, Henry Francis Lyte. The property remained in the possession of the Lyte family until 1949 when it became the Berry Head Hotel. Photographer Farnham Maxwell-Lyte also lived in the building and Evelyn George Martin, a sailor and cricketer, was a guest of the Lyte family in school holidays while at Eton College. In May 2013 a plaque was unveiled which commemorated Martin's time spent at the house.

The seaside town of **Paignton** forms part of Torbay and is a popular holiday destination on this part of the English Riviera.

A steam train passing by Goodrington Sands. The beach is very popular with holidaymakers visiting Paignton.

It was originally the home to a Celtic settlement and was first recorded in 1086 in the Domesday book. Its name was previously written as Peynton which derived from Paega's town, the original Anglo-Saxon settlement. In 1294, Paignton was given the status of a borough and had an annual market and fair. It grew into a small fishing village leading to a new harbour being built in 1847. The area was connected to the railway in 1859 which connected Paignton to Torquay as well as to London.

In the 1870s Oldway Mansion was built for Isaac Merritt Singer who had made his fortune from improvements he'd designed to improve sewing machines. Torbay Council later occupied the building, but in 2012 the site was developed into a hotel and retirement apartments.

The area thrived due to the tourism industry which was boosted by the opening of the railway line. The pier was constructed in 1879 and was designed by George Soudon Bridgman who also designed Oldway Mansion. The pier stretched 780ft and proved a popular destination for tourists. The tramway was extended into Paignton in 1911 but closed in 1934. In 1967 the Festival Theatre opened on the seafront which staged huge summer shows. It became a multi-screen cinema in 1999.

Nearby places of interest:
Paignton Zoo is located at Totnes Road in Paignton and contains over 2,000 animals. The park covers 80 acres and, as well as a large variety of animals, includes restaurants and cafés and interactive events such as Baboon Breakfast, Swamp Explorer and Pelican Picnic. Phone: 01803 697500.

Paignton Pier has rides and games for children including a bouncy castle, bumper cars, a Helter Skelter, arcade games as well as an ice cream parlour and café. The pier is located at Paignton Sands. Phone: 01803 522139.

Torquay adjoins Paignton which lies to its west. The town grew through two industries: fishing and agriculture. In the early 1800s Paignton became a fashionable holiday resort and was visited by members of the Royal Navy who had been fighting in the Napoleonic Wars. Popular with Victorian society and renowned for its healthy climate, it became known as the English Riviera. The author Agatha Christie was born in the town.

The area has been inhabited since Paleolithic times and hand axes discovered in Kents Cavern date back 40,000 years. A maxilla fragment found there is possible the oldest example of a modern human in Europe and dates back to approximately 37,000 to 40,000 years ago.

When Britain was part of the Roman Empire the area was visited by Roman soldiers who left offerings at a rock formation known as 'The Face' in Kents Cavern. However, no trace of a Roman settlement in Torquay has been found. Torre Abbey, a Premonstratensian monastery (a Roman Catholic order from Prémontré near Laon) was founded in 1196 and was the first major building in Torquay.

The harbour at Torquay which forms part of the English Riviera. The area has been popular with holidaymakers since Victorian times with visitor numbers increasing greatly with the introduction of the railway.

When the Torre railway station was opened on 18 December 1848 it resulted in rapid growth making the area a popular tourist destination. The main Torquay railway station opened on 2 August 1859 and had views out to sea from the platforms. In 1872, the town was granted borough status and began to attract summer visitors. Previously, it had been thought of as a convalescence retreat. In 1902 the first advertising campaign was launched to attract summer visitors and holidaymakers.

Nearby places of interest:
Kent's Cavern *features prehistoric caves once the home to ancient humans. Various events and activities take place throughout the year including guided tours and interactive displays. Phone: 01803 215136. Email: caves@kents-cavern.co.uk*

CHAPTER 8

Teignmouth to Sidmouth

Teignmouth first appeared in records in 1044 when it was called Tengemuða, which meant mouth of the stream. There were close by settlements long before this date and the banks of the Teign estuary were in Saxon hands from as early as 682AD. A record of a battle shows a conflict between Ancient Britons and Saxons in 927AD. Danish raids took place on the estuary during 1001.

Teignmouth was originally made up of two villages, East and West Teignmouth which were separated by the Tame, a stream which

Holidaymakers enjoying the sun beside the pier at Teignmouth. Teignmouth was originally called Tengemuða and first appeared in records in 1044. The name meant 'mouth of the stream'.

joined the Teign after travelling through marshland. The villages aren't mentioned in the Domesday book, however, East Teignbridge is recorded as being a market town in 1253 and West Teignbridge was granted the honour a few years later. Today the Tame runs in culverts beneath the town and is only visible at Brimley Brook where it is joined by smaller streams.

In the early fourteenth century Teignmouth was recorded as a major port, second only in Devon, to Dartmouth. In 1340 the town was attacked by the French and in 1347, seven ships and 120 men were sent to the expedition against Calais. The town became less important during the fifteenth century and was not recorded in the official record of 1577 probably due to the harbour silting up because of tin mining on Dartmoor.

In the seventeenth century Teignmouth suffered raids from the Dunkirkers, a group of Flemish privateers who attacked other Channel ports. Smuggling became important to local wealth as did cod fishing.

The French fleet anchored at Torbay in 1690 after the French Admiral Anne-Hilarion de Tourville achieved victory over an Anglo-Dutch fleet at the Battle of Beachy Head. Part of the fleet travelled up the coast and attacked Teignmouth. The attackers, who numbered approximately 1,000, burnt down the homes of 240 people, took away all their goods and destroyed ships, fishing boats, nets and other fishing craft. A collection of £11,000 was raised to aid the town and contributions came from as far away as churches in Yorkshire. The port was developed further due to the collection. The raid was the last attack on England and French Street records the occasion.

During the seventeenth and eighteenth centuries a windmill stood on the Den, once a large sand dune, but now a grassy area close to the seafront. However, in 1759 the windmill was removed. By the end of the 1700s, privateering was common and the trade was carried out in many other west country ports. The people of Teignmouth fitted out two privateers including the *Dragon* with sixteen guns and seventy

men and the *Bellona*, which carried sixteen guns, four cohorns
(mortars) and eight swivel guns. In September 1779, the *Bellona* set
sail on her first voyage but was lost when the ship overturned during
a violent storm off the Dawlish coast. Twenty-five crew members
were lost.

The fisheries at Newfoundland offered the main source of
employment to local men until the early 1800s. As the fishing
industry declined, tourism rose and a tea house was built on the Den
in 1787. By 1803 the town had become a fashionable watering place
and continued to be developed throughout the 1800s. Both of its
churches were rebuilt in 1815 and during the 1820s the first bridge
across the estuary linking to Shaldon was constructed. Also in the
1800s, George Templer's New Quay opened and the Esplanade, Den
Crescent and the central Assembly Rooms were prepared. In 1846 the
railway linked up to the town and twenty years later, the pier was built.

The First World War led to a disruption of many local businesses
when men left the town to enlist or were conscripted into the forces.
Over 175 men from Teignmouth lost their lives.

The town did not begin to recover until the 1920s when a golf
course opened at Little Haldon and the Morgan Giles shipbuilding
business commenced. Annual outings took employees and their
families on charabanc trips to nearby Dartmoor and other attractive
local destinations. The town was thriving by the 1930s and when the
nearby Haldon Aerodrome and School of Flying opened, Teignmouth
was described in adverts as the only south coast resort offering
aviation facilities.

In the Second World War Teignmouth suffered badly during air
raids and was bombed twenty-one times between July 1940 and
February 1944. Altogether, seventy-nine people were killed and
151 wounded. Approximately 228 houses were destroyed and a
further 2,000 were damaged during the attacks. On 8 May 1941 the
local hospital was bombed which led to the deaths of three nurses
and seven patients.

There was a plan by the US Navy to build a dam on the harbour so that a seaplane base could be set up. However, when the war progressed in favour of the allies, the plan was abandoned.

In September 1954, the hospital was rebuilt and became the first complete general hospital in the country to be constructed after the formation of the National Health Service.

Nearby places of interest:
The Teignmouth to Dawlish Railway Walk *allows ramblers to walk the South Devon Railway Sea Wall which includes one of Britain's most photographed stretches of railway line. There are magnificent views over Dawlish leading to Teignmouth's Eastcliff Park.*

The Teignmouth and Shaldon Museum *is located at 29 French Street in Teignmouth and allows visitors the chance to explore the fascinating history of the area. There are also regular events, concerts and workshops held there. Phone: 01626 777041. Email: info@teignheritage.org.uk*

Following the coast leads to the town of **Dawlish.** Before people settled there fishermen and salt makers travelled to the area to build salterns to make salt which was stored in nearby sheds. Dawlish water proved unpredictable during floods and led to nearby Teignmouth becoming a preferred site for salt-making. During the Anglo-Saxon period, between AD 400 and AD 1000, the practice stopped at Dawlish.

The earliest settlement grew up around where the parish church stands today. Early settlements are known to have existed at Aller Farm, Smallacombe, Lidwell and at Higher and Lower Southwood. In 1044 the area which now includes Dawlish was granted to Leofric, later the first Bishop of Exeter, by Edward the Confessor. Leofric gifted the land to the Diocese of Exeter after the Norman Conquest. It remained in their possession until it was sold in 1802.

The flowing water through the centre of Dawlish. During the 1700s, coastal locations in the south became popular with the rich, mainly due to George III making Weymouth his summer holiday residence in 1789.

During the 1700s coastal locations in the south became popular with the wealthy. This was mainly due to George III making Weymouth his summer holiday residence in 1789. During May 1795, the antiquarian and topographer, John Swete visited Dawlish and reported that, although it was previously no more than a fishing village, the area was now highly fashionable and accommodation was hard to find for a reasonable price.

During the early part of the 1800s, the land between the former settlement and the sea was landscaped, the stream straightened and small waterfalls were built into it. Beside it was a wide lawn and new houses were built. These made up The Strand on the north side and Brunswick Place on the south.

Isambard Kingdom Brunel constructed a railway in Dawlish during 1830. It ran on a pneumatic principle employing a 15-inch iron tube. One of the pumping stations was in Dawlish and the line travelled along the seafront. In 1802, Jane Austen visited Dawlish for a long holiday but later complained that its library was 'particularly pitiful and wretched'. Dawlish was mentioned several times in her 1811 novel *Sense and Sensibility*. It was also mentioned in Charles Dickens' book, *Nicholas Nickleby*, when the protagonist inherits a small farm nearby.

Nearby places of interest:
Dawlish Warren Beach *is a beautiful 'Blue Flag' family beach with sand dunes and small lakes which play host to a variety of wildlife. The beach stretches miles from Dawlish town towards the Exe estuary. During the summer months, there are free open-air events as well as children's entertainers and firework displays.*

Dawlish Warren Nature Reserve *covers 500 acres including grassland, sand dunes and mudflats. It is home to a variety of birdlife as well as over 600 different types of flowering plants. There is a visitor centre and guided walks can be arranged.*

Dawlish Museum *is located at the The Knowle in Barton Terrace and is packed with artefacts relating to Dawlish and the surrounding area. The museum has displays in eleven rooms over three floors. Their most famous exhibit is the display of Piper Bill Millins' D-Day bagpipes. Phone: 01626 888557. Email: info@dawlishmuseum.co.uk*

Lympstone lies on the eastern shore of the Exe estuary. The small village is popular with visitors. In medieval times, the area prospered due to farming and became a tourist destination during the early 1800s for well-off travellers. At one time cod fishing, whaling, boat and ship-building, river and inshore fishing for mackerel and salmon were popular sources of income. Burnt lime and coal were used to make fertilizer to enrich the soil of local farmers' fields.

The park at Exmouth. Byzantine coins dating back to 498–518AD, have been found on the nearby beach. They carried the mark of Anastasius I.

Ralph Lane, equerry to Queen Elizabeth I, was born in Lympstone. In 1585, he accompanied Sir Walter Raleigh on his second expedition to the New World. He founded a colony on Roanoke Island and was later present when the Spanish Armada was defeated.

The town of **Exmouth** lies on the east bank of the mouth of the River Exe. In 1970 Byzantine coins featuring the mark of Anastasius I and dating back to 498–518, were found on the beach. Exmouth was previously known as Lydwicnaesse in the eleventh century. Littleham and Withycombe Raleigh, the two ecclesiastical parishes which make up the town of Exmouth, can be traced back to before Saxon times.

The town began to grow in the thirteenth century. The land nearby was owned by Morin Uppehille who granted part of it to John the Miller who built a windmill there. He earned his living on the exposed point, aided by the prevailing wind. Together with the ferry

The promenade at Exmouth. In the eleventh century, the town was previously known as Lydwicnaesse. Littleham and Withycombe Raleigh, the two ecclesiastical parishes which make up the town of Exmouth, can be traced back to before Saxon times.

dock and a small settlement of farms the area eventually developed into Exmouth.

Sir Walter Raleigh left from Exmouth Harbour on many of his voyages during the 1500s. In the mid 1600s, the area came under attack from Turkish pirates who captured sailors and locals with the purpose of selling them into slavery on the North African coast. The practice took place all along the Devon and Cornwall coasts.

During the 1700s the town established itself as a holiday resort. Visitors who were unable to travel to Europe because of the French Revolution instead headed towards Devon. The medicinal salt waters were highly fashionable and a great attraction. Exmouth became popular with the rich who travelled to the town to recover from illness or to improve their health.

Deckchairs on the seafront at Sidmouth. The town is the gateway to the Jurassic Coast World Heritage Site and the remains of prehistoric fish, amphibians and reptiles have been found locally.

Well-known visitors included Lady Byron who travelled to the area with her daughter, Ada Lovelace. The town was also the home of Lady Nelson, the estranged wife of Lord Nelson, who is buried in Littleham Churchyard.

The rich continued to visit Exmouth and the area was exclusively their holiday destination until the railway opened in 1861, bringing with it mass tourism.

Sir Walter Raleigh was born at **Hayes Barton** which can be found on the edge of Woodbury Common, close to the village of **East Budleigh.**

Sidmouth, 14 miles east of Exeter, is the gateway to the Jurassic Coast World Heritage Site. Sidmouth is a major Triassic site, where the remains of prehistoric fish, amphibians and reptiles have been found. Today many specimens can be found in fallen blocks as well as in the cliffs. On the foreshore, bones and footprints of the Labyrinthodon lavisi, Mastodonsaurus, a Rhynchosaur and a Fodonyx spenceri have also been discovered.

The area appeared in the Domesday Book where it was referred to as 'Sedemuda'. This translated to 'mouth of the River Sid'. Like many coastal habitations, it made its living from fishing. Several attempts to build a harbour were made but none succeeded which limited the village as a port.

In the eighteenth and nineteenth centuries Sidmouth became a fashionable holiday resort and Georgian and Regency buildings still remain from this time.

In 1819 the Duke of Kent visited Woolbrook Glen for a few weeks. He was accompanied by his wife and baby daughter, who would later

The esplanade at Sidmouth. On the foreshore at Sidmouth, bones and footprints of the Labyrinthodont, Mastodonsaurus lavisi and a Rhynchosaur and Fodonyx spenceri have been discovered.

become Queen Victoria. The Duke died shortly after returning home. The place where he stayed later became the Royal Glen Hotel where a plaque records his visit.

Sidmouth was connected to the main railway network in 1874 which made the area a more accessible holiday destination.

Nearby places of interest:

The Donkey Sanctuary *at Sidmouth is home to hundreds of rescued donkeys. Admission and parking is free although donations are always welcome. The sanctuary opens 365 days a year. Phone: 01395 578222*

Connaught Gardens *are located at Peak Hill Road in Sidmouth and are open between 8.30am and 5pm. They feature a wide variety of plants as well as a café and offer stunning views of the sea and the red cliffs of Sidmouth. Phone: 01395 517528. Email: streetscene@ eastdevon.gov.uk*

Jacobs Ladder Beach *is a pebble beach reached from Connaught Gardens down a series of wooden steps. It is popular with families and has a nearby café.*

Peak Hill Llamas *allows visitors to walk with llamas along the Jurassic cliff coast path. They are based on a 330 acre working farm just outside Sidmouth. Bed and breakfast is available on the farm and afternoon walks end with a Devon Cream Tea. Phone: 01395 578697. E-mail: info@walkingwithllamas.co.uk*

Sidmouth Museum *is based in a Regency cottage covering two floors of displays and exhibits including fossils from the Jurassic Coast and reptile footprints found in Sidmouth. It is located at Hope Cottage, Church Street. Phone: 01395 516139. Email: sidmouth@ devonmuseums.net*

Acknowledgements

Thanks to Paul Willis (Worthing Wanderer) for letting me use some of his excellent photos, taken on his walks around the south coast of Devon, within the pages of this book. His Flickr website can be found at www.flickr.com/photos/worthingwanderer and his popular blog at http://worthingwanderer.blogspot.co.uk/

Other photos have been taken by myself and the older photos come from my own collection and from copyright-free sources such as Wikipedia. The photo of Torquay harbour was taken by Wikipedia user ianmacm and the photo of Kingsbridge quay and memorial by Wikipedia user stickman.

Thanks also to Tina Cole and Tilly Barker.

Bibliography

Books

Dartmoor Through the Year by Derek Tait (Amberley Publishing 2013).

Devon Through Time by Derek Tait (Amberley Publishing 2012).

Images of Plymouth: Stonehouse by Derek Tait (Driftwood Coast Publishing 2011).

Plymouth at War by Derek Tait (The History Press 2006).

Plymouth Hoe by Derek Tait (Driftwood Coast Publishing 2008).

Plymouth's Historic Barbican by Chris Robinson (Pen and Ink 2007).

Plymouth Tales from the Past (Driftwood Coast Publishing 2011).

Plymouth Through Time by Derek Tait (Amberley Publishing 2010).

River Tamar Through the Year by Derek Tait (Amberley Publishing 2012).

River Tamar Through Time by Derek Tait (Amberley Publishing 2011).

Saltash Passage by Derek Tait (Driftwood Coast Publishing 2006).

Websites

Adventure Clydesdale at www.adventureclydesdale.com

Ashburton Museum at www.ashburton.org/museum.htm

Babbacombe Model Village at www.model-village.co.uk

Blackpool Sands at www.blackpoolsands.co.uk

Bolberry Down at www.nationaltrust.org.uk/bolberry-down

Bradley Manor House at www.nationaltrust.org.uk/bradley

Britannia Royal Naval College at www.royalnavy.mod.uk/our-organisation/where-we-are/training-establishments/brnc-dartmouth

Buckfast Abbey at www.buckfast.org.uk

Buckfastleigh Butterfly Farm and Otter Sanctuary at www. ottersandbutterflies.co.uk

Buckland Abbey at www.nationaltrust.org.uk/buckland-abbey

Chris Robinson's Plymouth Prints at www.chrisrobinson.co.uk

Church House Inn at www.thechurchhouseinn.co.uk

Coleton Fishacre at www.nationaltrust.org.uk/coleton-fishacre

Connaught Gardens at www.eastdevon.gov.uk/parks-gardens-and-recreation/parks-and-gardens/connaught-gardens-sidmouth/history-of-connaught-gardens

Cremyll Ferry at www.plymouthboattrips.co.uk/ferries/cremyll-ferry

Dartmoor Hawking Falconry Experience at www.dartmoorhawking.co.uk

Dartmoor Prison Museum at www.dartmoor-prison.co.uk

Dartmoor Zoo at www.dartmoorzoo.org.uk

Dartmouth Castle at www.english-heritage.org.uk/visit/places/dartmouth-castle

Dartmouth Museum at www.dartmouthmuseum.org

Dawlish Museum at www.devonmuseums.net/Dawlish-Museum/Devon-Museums

Dawlish Warren Beach at www.dawlishwarren.com

Dawlish Warren Nature Reserve at www.dawlishwarren.info/see-dawlish-warren/nature-reserve

Dolphin Inn at www.visitplymouth.co.uk/food-and-drink/the-dolphin-inn-p1421363

Donkey Sanctuary (Ivybridge) at www.thedonkeysanctuary.org.uk/visit-us/ivybridge?gclid=CJWB-L_LodQCFYcV0wode8sLJw

The Donkey Sanctuary (Sidmouth) at www.thedonkeysanctuary.org.uk/visit-us/sidmouth

Elizabethan House at www.plymhearts.org/elizabethan-house

Elliot Terrace at www.plymouth.gov.uk/aboutcouncil/lordmayor/elliotterrace

Endsleigh Garden Centre at www.wyevalegardencentres.co.uk/stores/endsleigh-2255

Fast Rabbit Garden at www.fastrabbitfarm.co.uk

Garden House at www.thegardenhouse.org.uk

Greenway at www.nationaltrust.org.uk/greenway

Harbour House at www.harbourhouse.org.uk

Hill House Nursery and Garden at www.hillhousenursery.com

History of Plympton Castle at www.castlesfortsbattles.co.uk/south_
west/plympton_castle.html

House of Marbles at www.houseofmarbles.com

Ivybridge heritage at www.ivybridge-heritage.org

Jacobs Ladder Beach at www.thebeachguide.co.uk/south-west-
england/devon/jacobs-ladder-sidmouth.htm

Kents Cavern at www.kents-cavern.co.uk

Kingsbridge and District Light Railway at www.kdlr.co.uk

Mayflower Steps at www.mayflowersteps.co.uk

Merchant's House at www.plymhearts.org/merchants-house

Moretonhampstead Motor Museum at www.moretonmotormuseum.
co.uk

National Marine Aquarium at www.national-aquarium.co.uk

National Park Visitor Centre at www.dartmoor.gov.uk/visiting/
vi-planningyourvisit/vi-infocentres/vi-highmoorlandcentre

Old Ashburton at www.oldashburton.co.uk/conflict.php

Overbecks Museum and Garden at www.nationaltrust.org.uk/overbecks

Paignton Pier at www.paigntonpier.co.uk

Paignton Zoo at www.paigntonzoo.org.uk

Peak Hill Llamas at www.walkingwithllamas.co.uk

Pennywell Farm and Wildlife Centre at www.pennywellfarm.co.uk

Pixieland at www.pixieland.co.uk

Plym Railway at www.plymrail.co.uk

Plymouth Gin Distillery at www.plymouthdistillery.com

Plympton info at www.plympton.info/history.htm

Plympton St Maurice at www.plymptonstmaurice.com

Powdermills Pottery at www.powdermillspottery.com/acatalog/
home.html

River Dart Country Park at www.riverdart.co.uk

Royal William Yard at www.royalwilliamyard.com

St Andrew's Church (Ipplepen) at www.missioncommunity.org.uk

St Werburgh's Church at www.wemburychurch.co.uk

Salcombe Distilling Company at www.salcombegin.com

Salcombe Maritime Museum at www.salcombemuseum.org.uk

Saltram at www.nationaltrust.org.uk/saltram

Sidmouth   Museum   at   www.jurassiccoast.org/discovering/
    sidmouth-museum

Smeaton's Tower at www.visitplymouth.co.uk/things-to-do/smeatons-
    tower-p258003

South Devon Steam Railway at www.southdevonrailway.co.uk

South West Image Bank at www.southwestimagebank.com

Stover Canal at www.stovercanal.co.uk

Stover Country Park at www.new.devon.gov.uk/stovercountrypark

Tavistock Farmers Market at www.tavistockfarmersmarket.com

Tavistock Museum at www.tavistockmuseum.co.uk

Tavistock Pannier Market at www.tavistock.gov.uk/council-services/
    pannier-market

Tavistock Trout Farm and Fishery at www.tavistocktroutfishery.co.uk

Teignmouth and Shaldon Museum at www.teignheritage.org.uk

Teignmouth to Dawlish Railway Walk at www.southwestcoastpath.
    org.uk/walksdb/265

Thorn House and Garden at www.thornhouse.co.uk

Tinside Lido at www.everyoneactive.com/centre/tinside-lido

Totnes   Castle   at   www.english-heritage.org.uk/visit/places/totnes-
    castle

Totnes Guildhall at www.totnestowncouncil.gov.uk/Guildhall_627.aspx

Totnes Museum at www.totnesmuseum.org

Trago Mills at www.trago.co.uk

Ugbrooke House at www.ugbrooke.co.uk

Valiant Soldier at www.valiantsoldier.org.uk

Wembury Bay Riding School at www.wemburybayridingschool.co.uk

Wembury Marine Centre at www.wemburymarinecentre.org

Woodlands Family Theme Park at www.woodlandspark.com

Index